30 DAYS TO UNDERSTANDING
THE BIBLE

30 DAYS TO UNDERSTANDING THE BIBLE

Published by Thomas Nelson, Inc., P.O. Box 141000, Nashville, Tennessee, 37214

Published in association with the literary agency of Wolgemuth & Associates, Inc.

Library of Congress Cataloging-in-Publication Data

Anders, Max E., 1947–
   30 days to understanding the Bible by Max E. Anders.
   p. cm.
   ISBN 0-9434-9726-4
   ISBN 0-8499-3575-X 1994 rev.
   ISBN 0-7852-0999-9   1998 rev.
   ISBN 1-4185-0014-3

   1. Bible—Introductions. I. Anders, Max E., 1947– 30 days to understanding the Bible. II. Title.
   BS475.2.A53 1988
   220.6′1—dc21   88-10818
                                                   CIP

1 2 3 4 5 6 7—09 08 07 06 05 04

Printed in the United States of America

*To Jake and Wilma,
my spiritual mentors and dear friends*

Conclusion

Appendix

INTRODUCTION

LET'S MAKE A BARGAIN.

If you'll give me fifteen minutes a day for thirty days, I'll give you an understanding of the Bible, the most widely distributed publication in history (approximately four billion copies). In one month, you'll learn the story of the entire Bible...

all the major men and women,

all the major events, and

all the major points of geography.

You will be able to put these people and facts together in their proper chronological order and trace the geographical movement as you think your way through the entire Bible!

Yet the Bible is more than history. It is a treasure-house of important teachings that have been the foundation of Western civilization from the Roman Empire until today, including important and profound ideas which have been embraced by Christians for the last 2,000 years. You will learn about the Ten Great Subjects of the Bible:

Bible	Man
God	Sin
Jesus	Salvation
Holy Spirit	Church
Angels	Future Things

No attempt has been made to interpret the Bible. The information is presented at face value as it is found in Scripture. No previous knowledge is assumed. A beginner will not be overwhelmed, and the established student will find much help organizing and expanding what he or she already knows.

The Bible is an enormous book covering much information and many subjects. It is not possible to learn everything about it in thirty days. But you can gain a beginning knowledge, an overview, that you can use to build a more complete understanding in the years ahead. In just fifteen minutes a day for thirty days, you can gain a foundational grasp of the most important book ever written.

Section One

The Story of the Old Testament

CHAPTER ONE

THE STRUCTURE OF THE BIBLE

 CHARLES STEINMETZ WAS AN ELECTRICAL ENGINEER OF towering intellect. After he retired, he was asked by a major appliance manufacturer to locate a malfunction in their electrical equipment. None of the manufacturer's experts had been able to locate the problem. Steinmetz spent some time walking around and testing the various parts of the machine complex. Finally, he took out of his pocket a piece of chalk and marked an X on a particular part of one machine. The manufacturer's people disassembled the machine, discovering to their amazement that the defect lay precisely where Steinmetz's chalk mark was located.

Some days later, the manufacturer received a bill from Steinmetz for ten thousand dollars. They protested the amount and asked him to itemize it. He sent back an itemized bill:

Making one chalk mark $ 1
Knowing where to place it $ 9,999

If you know where the chalk marks go, the most overwhelming tasks are easily solved. If you don't, even simple tasks can be impossible.

Learning about the Bible can be much the same. If you don't know much about it, it can be like trying to cross the Sahara Desert blindfolded. Yet if you learn where a few of the major chalk marks go, the Bible can be at the very least an interesting and valuable source of information and inspiration.

My own experience bears this out. Many years ago, I decided I was going to master the Bible. I was going to begin with Genesis and read through Revelation, and I wasn't going to put it down until I understood it. I soon became hopelessly entangled in a jungle of fantastic stories, unpronounceable names, broken plots, unanswered questions, and endless genealogies. I stubbed my toe on Leviticus, sprained my ankle on Job, hit my head on Ecclesiastes, and fell headlong into the mud on Habakkuk.

I was defeated. I threw my Bible down, concluding that the Bible was a series of unrelated stories put together in random order!

Then one day I discovered a key. With this key, the fog that enshrouded my understanding of the Bible began to lift. Not that things came into sharp focus, but at least I began to see shapes on the horizon.

The key: *Learning the structure of the Bible*. If you want to learn architecture, you must first learn how buildings are put together. If you want to learn sailing, you must first learn how ships are put together. And if you want to learn to understand the Bible, you must first learn how the Bible is put together.

THE OLD AND NEW TESTAMENTS

The Bible has two major divisions: the Old Testament and the New Testament. The Old Testament begins with creation and tells the story of the Jewish people up to the time of Christ. It is made up of *thirty-nine* individual "books" (the Book of Genesis, the Book of Exodus, etc.) written by twenty-eight different authors and spans a period of over two thousand years.

The New Testament is the record of the birth of Jesus, His life and ministry, and the ministry of His disciples, which was carried on after Jesus was crucified. The New Testament is composed of *twenty-seven* books written by nine different authors and covers a time period of less than one hundred years. The total number of books in the entire Bible is *sixty-six*.

SELF-TEST

How many?   _39_____ books in the Old Testament
              _27_____ books in the New Testament
              _66_____ books in the whole Bible

OLD TESTAMENT BOOKS

Genesis	2 Chronicles	Daniel
Exodus	Ezra	Hosea
Leviticus	Nehemiah	Joel
Numbers	Esther	Amos
Deuteronomy	Job	Obadiah
Joshua	Psalms	Jonah
Judges	Proverbs	Micah
Ruth	Ecclesiastes	Nahum
1 Samuel	Song of Solomon	Habakkuk
2 Samuel	Isaiah	Zephaniah
1 Kings	Jeremiah	Haggai
2 Kings	Lamentations	Zechariah
1 Chronicles	Ezekiel	Malachi

NEW TESTAMENT BOOKS

Matthew	Ephesians	Hebrews
Mark	Philippians	James
Luke	Colossians	1 Peter
John	1 Thessalonians	2 Peter
Acts	2 Thessalonians	1 John
Romans	1 Timothy	2 John
1 Corinthians	2 Timothy	3 John
2 Corinthians	Titus	Jude
Galatians	Philemon	Revelation

THE OLD TESTAMENT

Here is the key to understanding the Old Testament. Of the thirty-nine books in the Old Testament, *there are three different kinds of books:* Historical Books, Poetical Books, and Prophetical Books.

What kind of information would you expect to find in the Historical Books? ....*history!*
What kind of information would you expect to find in the Poetical Books?..*poetry!*
What kind of information would you expect to find in the Prophetical Books? ....*prophecy!*

If you know what kind of book you are reading, then you will know what kind of information to expect, and you can easily follow the logical flow of the Old Testament!

In the Old Testament:

. . . the first seventeen books are historical,
. . . the next five books are poetical, and
. . . the next seventeen books are prophetical!

THE THREE KINDS OF BOOKS IN THE OLD TESTAMENT

Historical	Poetical	Prophetical
Genesis	Job	Isaiah
Exodus	Psalms	Jeremiah
Leviticus	Proverbs	Lamentations
Numbers	Ecclesiastes	Ezekiel
Deuteronomy	Song of Solomon	Daniel
Joshua		Hosea
Judges		Joel
Ruth		Amos
1 Samuel		Obadiah
2 Samuel		Jonah
1 Kings		Micah
2 Kings		Nahum
1 Chronicles		Habakkuk
2 Chronicles		Zephaniah
Ezra		Haggai
Nehemiah		Zechariah
Esther		Malachi

If you want to read the story of the Hebrew nation in the Old Testament, you must read the first seventeen books. These books compose a historical time line for the nation of Israel.

If you want to read the poetry of Israel, you must read the next five books of the Old Testament.

If you want to read about the prophecy of Israel, you must read the final seventeen books.

This is somewhat oversimplified, because there is some poetry in the Historical Books, and some history in the Prophetical Books, etc. The point is, however, that each of the books fits into a primary category. If you keep this structure in mind, the Old Testament will begin to take shape for you.

My mistake was in assuming that the whole Old Testament was one long, unbroken story and that the history would flow evenly and consistently out of one book into the next until they were all finished. Now I know the story line is contained in the first seventeen books.

Of the seventeen Historical Books, eleven are *primary* Historical Books and six are *secondary* Historical Books. The history of Israel is advanced in the eleven primary books and repeated or amplified in the six secondary books. The Poetical and Prophetical Books were written during the time period that is constructed in the first seventeen books.

Let's take a look at the historical time line of the Old Testament in chart form:

TIME LINE OF THE OLD TESTAMENT

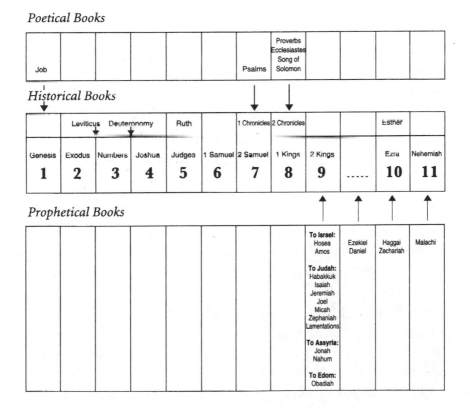

As you can see, Job was written during the time period of the Book of Genesis, and Psalms during the time of 2 Samuel, while Proverbs, Ecclesiastes, and Song of Solomon were written during the time of 1 Kings, and so on.

To use an analogy, we constructed a similar chart for U.S. history. Imagine that you read an American history book for the main story line. The history book would give you the major periods in U.S. history. Some of these periods might be associated with a major poet or writer and a major philosopher. The poets would correspond to the poets of Israel, and the philosophers would correspond to the biblical prophets.

TIME LINE OF U.S. HISTORY

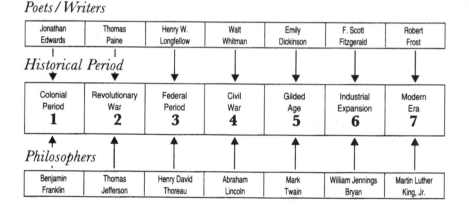

Poets / Writers

| Jonathan Edwards | Thomas Paine | Henry W. Longfellow | Walt Whitman | Emily Dickinson | F. Scott Fitzgerald | Robert Frost |

Historical Period

| Colonial Period **1** | Revolutionary War **2** | Federal Period **3** | Civil War **4** | Gilded Age **5** | Industrial Expansion **6** | Modern Era **7** |

Philosophers

| Benjamin Franklin | Thomas Jefferson | Henry David Thoreau | Abraham Lincoln | Mark Twain | William Jennings Bryan | Martin Luther King, Jr. |

THE NEW TESTAMENT

Of the twenty-seven books of the New Testament, *there are also three different kinds of books:* Historical Books, Pauline Epistles, and General Epistles. The Historical Books are the four Gospels and the Acts of the Apostles. The Epistles were letters written to various individuals and church congregations. The Pauline Epistles were letters written by the apostle Paul. The General Epistles were letters written to individuals and congregations by a number of different people, hence the rather generic name General Epistles. The primary content in all the Epistles is instruction on Christian doctrine and lifestyle.

What kind of information would you expect to find in the Historical Books? ....*history!*
What kind of information would you expect to find in the Pauline Books? ....*instruction!*
What kind of information would you expect to find in the General Epistles? ....*instruction!*

In the New Testament:

. . . the first five books are Historical Books,

. . . the next thirteen books are Pauline Epistles, and

. . . the next nine books are General Epistles!

THE THREE KINDS OF BOOKS IN THE NEW TESTAMENT

Historical	*Pauline*	*General*
Matthew	**TO CHURCHES:**	Hebrews
Mark		James
Luke	Romans	1 Peter
John	1 Corinthians	2 Peter
Acts	2 Corinthians	1 John
	Galatians	2 John
	Ephesians	3 John
	Philippians	Jude
	Colossians	Revelation
	1 Thessalonians	
	2 Thessalonians	
	TO INDIVIDUALS:	
	1 Timothy	
	2 Timothy	
	Titus	
	Philemon	

If you want to read the story of Jesus and the Church He established, you must read the first five books of the New Testament. These five books form the historical framework for understanding the entire New Testament!

If you want to read the apostle Paul's instruction to churches and individuals, you must read the next thirteen books.

If you want to read the instruction to churches and individuals by men like the apostles Peter and John, you must read the final nine books of the New Testament.

REFERENCES

To find something in the Bible, you use a standard reference system. This consists of the name of the book of the Bible, the chapter number followed by a colon, and the verse number (each chapter is divided into numbered verses). For example:

Genesis 1:1 =   Genesis   1:   1
                (book)   (chapter) (verse)

When you see a reference such as Joshua 1:21, you will either have to memorize the books of the Bible to know where Joshua is, or you can look it up in the table of contents. It is well worth the time to memorize the books, and it is easiest to memorize them according to their categories.

For example, you now know that there are three types of books in both the Old Testament (Historical, Poetical, and Prophetical) and the New Testament (Historical, Pauline Epistles, and General Epistles), and how many books are in each section. Memorize the first seventeen Historical Books. Then, when you have these memorized, learn the five Poetical Books, and so on. This system is much easier than attempting to memorize an unbroken list of sixty-six books.

There is no substitute for reading the whole book for yourself, of course, but it is possible to offer a quick overview. To read "The Story of the Bible," turn to the Appendix.

SUMMARY

1. There are 39 books in the Old Testament.
    There are 27 books in the New Testament.
    There are 66 books in the whole Bible.

2. The Old Testament is the story of God and the Hebrew people, their poets, and prophets.

There are 3 kinds of books in the Old Testament:

17 Historical Books,
 5 Poetical Books, and
17 Prophetical Books.

3. The New Testament is the story of Jesus of Nazareth, the Church He founded, and its growth under the leadership of His apostles after His death.

There are 3 kinds of books in the New Testament:

 5 Historical Books,
13 Pauline Epistles, and
 9 General Epistles.

SELF-TEST

The Bible:
How many?

_39_ books in the Old Testament
_27_ books in the New Testament
_66_ books in the whole Bible

The Old Testament:
The Old Testament is the story of G_od_ and the H_ebrew_ people, their poets, and prophets.

There are 3 kinds of books in the Old Testament:

H _istorical_ Books,
P _oetical_ Books, and
P _rophetical_ Books.

There are ___17___ Historical Books.
There are ___5___ Poetical Books.
There are ___17___ Prophetical Books.

The New Testament:

The New Testament is the story of J*esus*, the C*hurch* He founded, and its growth under the leadership of His a*postle*s after His death.

There are 3 kinds of books in the New Testament:

H*istorical* Books,
P*auline* Epistles, and
General Epistles.

There are _____5_____ Historical Books.
There are ____13____ Pauline Epistles. *9 to Churches*
There are _____9_____ General Epistles. *4 to people*

Congratulations! You are off to a fine start. As we move from the general to the specific, you can build your knowledge of the Bible like rows of brick on a house. In twenty-nine more days, your house will be finished.

CHAPTER TWO

THE GEOGRAPHY OF THE OLD TESTAMENT

THE SIZE OF OUR SOLAR SYSTEM IS BEYOND COMPREHENSION. To get some perspective, imagine you are in the middle of the Bonneville Salt Flats with nothing but tabletop flat ground around you for miles and miles. There you put down a beachball two feet in diameter, which you use to represent the sun. To get a feel for the immensity of the solar system, walk about a city block and put down a mustard seed for the first planet, Mercury. Go another block and for Venus put down an ordinary BB. Mark off yet another block and put down a green pea to represent Earth. A final block from there, put down a mustard seed to represent Mars. Then sprinkle some grass seed around for an asteroid belt.

We have now walked about four blocks, and we have a beachball (sun), mustard seed (Mercury), BB (Venus), pea (Earth), mustard seed (Mars), and grass seed (asteroid belt). Now things begin to stretch out.

Continue for another quarter of a mile. Place an orange on the ground for Jupiter. Walk another third of a mile and put down a golf ball for Saturn.

Now lace up your tennis shoes and check their tread. Then step off another mile and, for Uranus, drop a marble. Go another mile and place a cherry there for Neptune. Finally, walk for another two miles and put down another marble for Pluto.

At last, go up in an airplane and look down. On a smooth surface almost ten miles in diameter we have a beach ball, a mustard seed, a BB, a pea, another mustard seed, some grass seed, an orange, a golf ball, a marble, a cherry, and another marble.

To understand our replica of the solar system even better, use another beachball to represent Alpha Centauri, the next-nearest star to our sun. You would have to go another 6,720 miles and put it down in Japan!

Understanding the size and location of things and the relationships and distances between them gives us perspective. Just as this example gives us perspective about the solar system, a knowledge of geography can give perspective about the events of the Bible. It is helpful to know the names, locations, and relative positions of important places. Otherwise, we skim over information without comprehension or visualization, and this makes the Bible less interesting and less easily understood.

The one who is ignorant of geography cannot know history. The Bible is largely history. So to begin our mastery of the history of the Bible, we must start with the geography of the Bible.

BODIES OF WATER

The primary anchor points for mastering the geography of the Bible are the bodies of water. *(As you read each description, go to the Work Map and insert the name of the body of water beside the matching number.)*

1. The Mediterranean Sea
The land of the Old Testament lies east of this beautiful blue body of water.

2. The Sea of Galilee
To call this body a sea seems to be an overstatement. It is a freshwater lake that is seven miles wide and fourteen miles long. It lies about thirty-six miles inland from the Mediterranean.

3. The Jordan River
Flowing south out of the Sea of Galilee, the Jordan River travels for sixty-five miles, as the crow flies, to empty into the Dead Sea. Many are surprised at how much history has revolved around such a small river.

4. The Dead Sea
Shaped like a giant hot dog with a bite out of the lower third, the Dead Sea lies at the "bottom of the world." It is the lowest point on land, almost three thousand feet below sea level at its

lowest point, so that water flows into it, but no water flows out of it. As a result, the water has a very high concentration of mineral deposits and does not support normal plant or animal life. Hence the name Dead Sea.

5. Nile River

Perhaps the most famous river in the world, the Nile flows through the heart of Egypt, spreads out like so many fingers, and empties into the waiting arms of the Mediterranean.

6. Tigris and (7.) Euphrates Rivers

These twin rivers flow for almost a thousand miles each before they join and flow into the Persian Gulf.

8. Persian Gulf

These last three bodies of water, the Tigris, the Euphrates, and the Persian Gulf, form the easternmost boundary for the lands of the Old Testament. The Tigris and Euphrates flow through present-day Iraq, while the Persian Gulf separates Iran from Saudi Arabia.

WORK MAP

Bodies of Water of the Old Testament

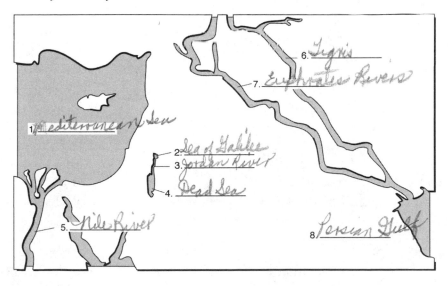

LOCATIONS

With the geographical framework offered by the bodies of water, we can establish the locations that are relevant to the Old Testament. *(As you read the description of each location, insert its name beside the appropriate letter on the Location Work Map that follows.)*

A. The Garden of Eden

The exact location of the Garden of Eden, where everything began, is impossible to pinpoint. However, it was near the convergence of four rivers, two of which were the Tigris and Euphrates.

B. Canaan/Israel/Palestine

This smallish piece of real estate, which lies between the Mediterranean coast and the Sea of Galilee-Jordan River-Dead Sea, changes names throughout the Old Testament. In Genesis it is called *Canaan*. After the Hebrew people establish themselves in the land in the Book of Joshua, it becomes known as *Israel*. Thirteen hundred years later, at the beginning of the New Testament, it is called *Palestine*.

C. Jerusalem

Located just off the northwestern shoulder of the Dead Sea, this city, nestled in the central mountains of Israel, is so central to the story of the Old Testament that it must be singled out and identified. It is the capital of the nation of Israel.

D. Egypt

The *grande dame* of ancient civilization, Egypt plays a central role in the history of the Old Testament.

E. Assyria

Located at the headwaters of the Tigris and Euphrates, this great world power is notable in the Old Testament for conquering the Northern Kingdom of Israel and dispersing her people to the four winds.

F. Babylonia

Another gigantic historical world power, this fabulous, albeit short-lived, nation conquered Assyria. It also conquered the Southern Kingdom of Judah 136 years after Assyria conquered the

Northern Kingdom of Israel. It is found in Mesopotamia, between the Tigris and Euphrates. (Mesopotamia means "in the middle of" [meso]—"rivers" [potamus].)

G. Persia

The final historical superpower of the Old Testament is located at the north bank of the Persian Gulf. Persia comes into play by conquering Babylonia and by allowing the Hebrews to return from captivity in Babylonia to rebuild the city of Jerusalem and reinstate temple worship.

If these historical notes are foreign to you, don't worry about it now. Instead, content yourself with learning these locations so that, as the story unfolds, the names of these locations will mean something to you.

LOCATION WORK MAP

Locations of the Old Testament

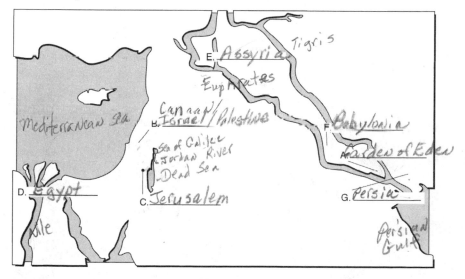

Now compare the ancient map you have just filled in with the following contemporary map of the same region.

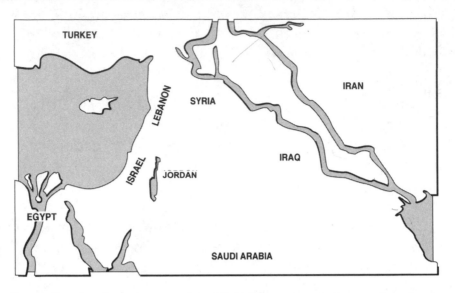

It might also help to get this Old Testament information into perspective by seeing how the map of the Old Testament compares with an overlay of a map of the state of Texas.

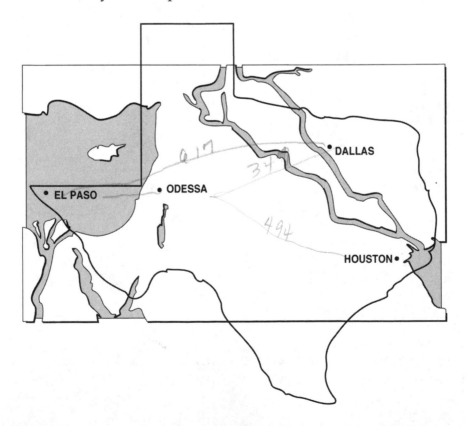

The entire land of the Old Testament is approximately the same size as the state of Texas. Traveling from the Persian Gulf to Israel would be like going from Houston to Odessa. Traveling from Israel to Egypt would be like going from Odessa to El Paso. If you keep this in mind as the story of the Bible unfolds, it will help you keep geographical perspective.

REVIEW

The Geography of the Old Testament

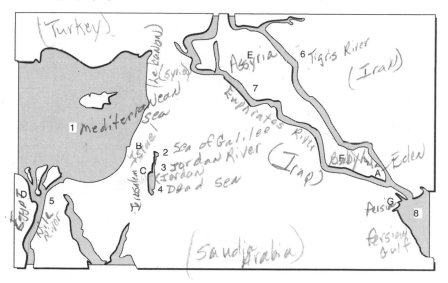

Review the eight bodies of water and the seven locations by placing the numbers and letters by the appropriate names below.

BODIES OF WATER
- *1* Mediterranean Sea
- *2* Sea of Galilee
- *3* Jordan River
- *4* Dead Sea
- *5* Nile River
- *6* Tigris River
- *7* Euphrates River
- *8* Persian Gulf

LOCATIONS
- *A* Eden
- *B* Israel
- *C* Jerusalem
- *D* Egypt
- *E* Assyria
- *F* Babylonia
- *G* Persia

SELF-TEST

The Geography of the Old Testament

As the final exercise, fill in the blanks from memory. (*Remember, the blanks with numbers are bodies of water, and the blanks with letters are locations.*)

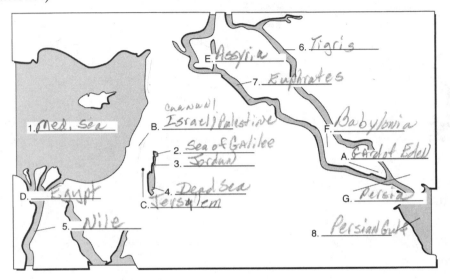

Excellent! Your knowledge of the geography of the Old Testament will enable you to understand and envision the history that unfolds from it. You have just mastered an important section.

ANSWERS

The Geography of the Old Testament

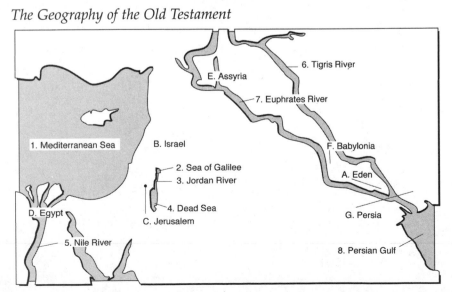

THE HISTORICAL BOOKS

ON THE FLIGHT FROM LOS ANGELES TO PORTLAND, ONE FLIES over the entire length of the Cascade Mountains. From thirty-five thousand feet it is difficult to get the perspective to determine which are the higher mountain peaks.

One day in late October as I was making that flight, the air was crisp and clear after a light snowfall and the puzzle of how to differentiate the higher from the lower peaks was answered. The snow only fell on elevations of about seven thousand feet and higher. As we flew over them, regardless of how close or far away they were, the highest peaks were easy to determine: they were the ones with snow on them.

As we begin to look into the stories of the Old Testament, we will only look at the highest peaks, the ones with snow on them.

To do so, it will be helpful to continue the analogy with the story of the United States. If you were going to condense just the story of the United States, omitting the poets and philosophers, you would take the main periods of history, link them with the central historic figure of the era, and add the primary location. In chart form, it might look like this:

TIME LINE OF U.S. HISTORY

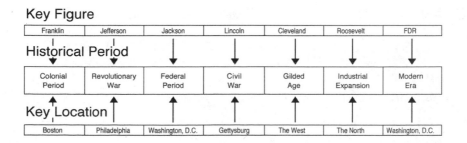

Key Figure

Franklin	Jefferson	Jackson	Lincoln	Cleveland	Roosevelt	FDR

Historical Period

Colonial Period	Revolutionary War	Federal Period	Civil War	Gilded Age	Industrial Expansion	Modern Era

Key Location

Boston	Philadelphia	Washington, D.C.	Gettysburg	The West	The North	Washington, D.C.

Include a brief story line summary of the era, and the story of the United States could be overviewed in a chart, such as the following:

STORY OF THE UNITED STATES

KEY ERA	KEY FIGURE	LOCATION	STORY LINE
Colonial	*Franklin*	*Boston*	As the thirteen colonies long for independence, Franklin leads in the formulation of necessary strategy.
Revolution	*Jefferson*	*Philadelphia*	Jefferson writes the Declaration of Independence.
Etc.	*Etc.*	*Etc.*	Etc.

This same approach can be used in condensing the story of the Bible, charting the main periods (or eras), the central figures, the main locations, and a summary story line. The story line of the Bible can be divided into twelve main eras, with a central figure and main location for each era. Nine of the eras are found in the Old Testament, and three are found in the New Testament.

In this chapter, we will deal with only the Old Testament and will complete only the first three aspects of the chart: the main eras, the central figures, and the main locations. The summary story line and the New Testament events will be added in the following chapters.

THE NINE MAIN ERAS OF THE OLD TESTAMENT

1. **Creation**
   The *creation* of the world and man, and early events.

2. **Patriarch**
   The birth of the Hebrew people through a family of *patriarchs*, covering a period of two hundred years.

3. Exodus

The *exodus* of the Hebrew people as they are delivered out of four hundred years of slavery in Egypt.

4. Conquest

The *conquest* of the Promised Land by the Hebrew people upon their return from Egypt.

5. Judges

A four-hundred-year period during which Israel is governed by rulers called *judges*.

6. Kingdom

An additional four-hundred-year period during which Israel becomes a full-fledged nation ruled by a *monarchy*.

7. Exile

A seventy-year period during which Israel's leaders live in *exile*, having been conquered by foreign countries.

8. Return

The *return* of exiled Jews to Jerusalem to rebuild the city and the temple.

9. Silence

A final four-hundred-year period between the close of the Old Testament and the opening of the New Testament.

Following the pattern of the chart for the Story of the United States, let's begin to chart the Story of the Old Testament.

STORY OF THE OLD TESTAMENT

ERA	FIGURE	LOCATION	STORY LINE
Creation *Patriarch* *Exodus* *Conquest* *Judges* *Kingdom* *Exile* *Return* *Silence*	To be supplied later	To be supplied later	To be supplied later

Another way to help us remember the historical story line of the Bible is to visualize the main eras with symbols, such as in the Arc of Bible History.

ARC OF BIBLE HISTORY

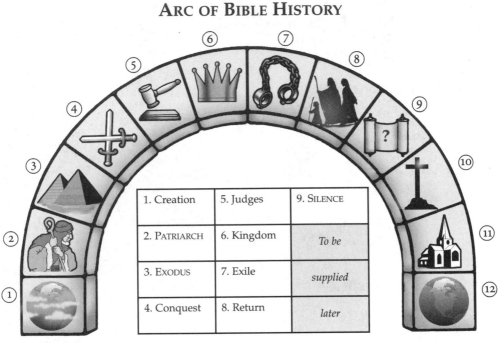

1. Creation	5. Judges	9. SILENCE
2. PATRIARCH	6. Kingdom	To be
3. EXODUS	7. Exile	supplied
4. Conquest	8. Return	later

REVIEW

Write in the correct era on the line matching the description.

OPTIONS:
Exile
Judges
Creation
Kingdom
Patriarch
Conquest
Return
Silence
Exodus

ERA:

Creation

Patriarch

Exodus

DESCRIPTION:

The *creation* of the world and man, and early events

The birth of the Hebrew people through a family of *patriarchs*, covering a period of two hundred years

The *exodus* of the Hebrew people as they are delivered out of four hundred years of slavery in Egypt

OPTIONS:	ERA:	DESCRIPTION:
	Conquest	The *conquest* of the Promised Land by the Hebrew people upon their return from Egypt
	Judges	A four-hundred-year period during which Israel is governed by rulers called *judges*
	Kingdom	An additional four-hundred-year period during which Israel becomes a full-fledged nation ruled by a *monarchy*
	Exile	A seventy-year period during which Israel's leaders live in *exile*, having been conquered by foreign countries
	Return	The *return* of the exiled Jews to Jerusalem to rebuild the city and the temple
	Silence	A final four-hundred-year period between the close of the Old Testament and the opening of the New Testament

THE NINE CENTRAL FIGURES OF THE OLD TESTAMENT

ERA:	FIGURE:	DESCRIPTION:
Creation	Adam	The first *man*
Patriarch	Abraham	The first *patriarch*
Exodus	Moses	The leader of the *exodus*
Conquest	Joshua	The leader of Israel's *army*
Judges	Samson	The most famous *judge*
Kingdom	David	The most well-known Israelite *king*
Exile	Daniel	The major exilic *prophet*
Return	Ezra	The central *return* leader
Silence	Pharisees	The *religious* leaders

REVIEW

(Fill in the blank.)

ERA:	FIGURE:	DESCRIPTION:
Creation	Adam	The first _man_
Patriarch	Abraham	The first _patriarch_
Exodus	Moses	The leader of the _exodus_
Conquest	Joshua	The leader of Israel's _army_
Judges	Samson	The most famous _judge_
Kingdom	David	The most well-known Israelite _king_
Exile	Daniel	The major exilic _prophet_
Return	Ezra	The central _return_ leader
Silence	Pharisees	The _religious_ leaders

(Match the era with the key figure.)

ERA:	FIGURE:	OPTIONS:
Creation	_Adam_	Moses
Patriarch	_Abraham_	Daniel
Exodus	_Moses_	Abraham
Conquest	_Joshua_	Joshua
Judges	_Samson_	Pharisees
Kingdom	_David_	Ezra
Exile	_Daniel_	David
Return	_Ezra_	Samson
Silence	_Pharisees_	Adam

Now we will add the central figure to our story line chart.

STORY OF THE OLD TESTAMENT

ERA	FIGURE	LOCATION	STORY LINE
Creation	Adam		
Patriarch	Abraham		
Exodus	Moses		
Conquest	Joshua	To be	To be
Judges	Samson	supplied	supplied
Kingdom	David	later	later
Exile	Daniel		
Return	Ezra		
Silence	Pharisees		

Our final task is to identify the general or primary geographic location of the events of the main eras of the Old Testament. Beginning with Creation and Adam, as an exercise in memory, write in the name of each main era and its central historical figure as you read the description of the location of each of the eras.

THE NINE MAIN LOCATIONS OF THE OLD TESTAMENT

ERA:	FIGURE:	LOCATION:	DESCRIPTION:
1. *Creation*	*Adam*	Eden	The garden of Eden, where Adam is created. Near the convergence of the Tigris and Euphrates Rivers.
2. *Patriarchs*	*Abraham*	Canaan	Abraham migrates from Ur, near Eden, to Canaan, where he and the other patriarchs live until the time of slavery in Egypt.
3. *Exodus*	*Moses*	Egypt	During a severe famine, the Israelites migrate to Egypt and are enslaved four hundred years before their exodus to freedom.
4. *Conquest*	*Joshua*	Canaan	Joshua leads the conquest of the Promised Land in Canaan.
5. *Judges*	*Samson*	Canaan	The Israelites live in Canaan under a loose tribal system ruled by judges for the next four hundred years.
6. *Kingdom*	*David*	Israel	With the formation of a formal monarchy, the land is now referred to by the national name of *Israel*.

7. _Exile_   _Daniel_   Babylonia Because of judgment for national moral corruption, Israel is conquered by foreign nations, finally forcing her leaders into seventy years of exile in Babylonia.

8. _Return_   _Ezra_   Jerusalem The exiled Israelites are allowed to return to Jerusalem to rebuild the city and temple, though they remain under the dominion of Persia.

9. _Silence_   _Pharisees_ Jerusalem Though dominion of the land changes from Persia to Greece to Rome, Israel is allowed to worship in Jerusalem without disruption for the next four hundred years of "silence."

Along with the main era and the central figure, we are now able to add the main location to our chart.

STORY OF THE OLD TESTAMENT

ERA	FIGURE	LOCATION	STORY LINE
Creation	Adam	Eden	
Patriarch	Abraham	Canaan	
Exodus	Moses	Egypt	To be supplied later
Conquest	Joshua	Canaan	
Judges	Samson	Canaan	
Kingdom	David	Israel	
Exile	Daniel	Babylonia	
Return	Ezra	Jerusalem	
Silence	Pharisees	Jerusalem	

ARC OF BIBLE HISTORY

(Fill in the names of the eras. To check your answers, see the Appendix.)

1. Creation	5. Judges	9. Silence
2. Patriarch	6. Kingdom	10. Gospels
3. Exodus	7. Exile	11. Church
4. Conquest	8. Return	12. Mission

REVIEW

On the following map draw arrows to show the movement during the major Eras of the Old Testament that we have just learned. Begin at Eden and draw an arrow to the next location as it changes: Eden to Canaan, to Egypt, to Canaan, to Babylonia, to Jerusalem.

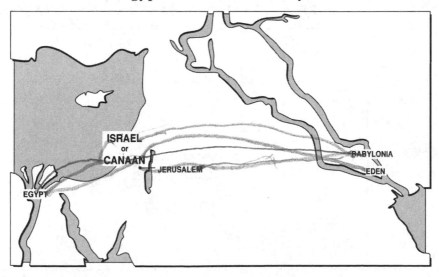

In its most basic form, your map should look something like this:

From the options given, fill in the blanks in the following chart, matching the location to the era and central figure. (*A location may be used more than once.*)

Babylonia   Eden   Israel

Canaan   Egypt   Jerusalem

STORY OF THE OLD TESTAMENT

ERA	FIGURE	LOCATION	STORY LINE
Creation	Adam	Eden	
Patriarch	Abraham	Canaan	
Exodus	Moses	Egypt	
Conquest	Joshua	Canaan	To be supplied later
Judges	Samson	Canaan	
Kingdom	David	Israel	
Exile	Daniel	Babylonia	
Return	Ezra	Jerusalem	
Silence	Pharisees	Jerusalem	

You are now ready to begin final mastery of a very critical chart. Once you master this chart, you have come a long way in understanding the overview of the Old Testament. Fill in the blanks.

STORY OF THE OLD TESTAMENT

ERA	FIGURE	LOCATION	STORY LINE
Creation	Adam	*Eden*	
Patriarch	*Abraham*	Canaan	
Exodus	Moses	Egypt	
Conquest	Joshua	*Canaan*	To be supplied later
Judges	*Samson*	Canaan	
Kingdom	David	Israel	
Exile	Daniel	*Babylonia*	
Return	*Ezra*	Jerusalem	
Silence	Pharisees	Jerusalem	

SELF-TEST

Finally, fill in the following chart from memory. It might be easiest to fill in the eras, then go back and fill in the central figures and main locations. (*To check your answers see the Appendix for a completed Story of the Bible chart.*)

STORY OF THE OLD TESTAMENT

ERA	FIGURE	LOCATION	STORY LINE
Creation	*Adam*	*Eden*	
Patriarch	*Abraham*	*Canaan*	
Exodus	*Moses*	*Egypt*	
Conquest	*Joshua*	*Canaan*	To be supplied later
Judges	*Samson*	*Canaan*	
Kingdom	*David*	*Israel*	
Exile	*Daniel*	*Babylonia*	
Return	*Ezra*	*Jerusalem*	
Silence	*Pharisees*	*Jerusalem*	

Congratulations! You have just taken a major step toward mastering an overview of the Old Testament. From now on, we will become more and more specific, but you have laid a good foundation that can be built upon in successive chapters.

CHAPTER FOUR

THE CREATION ERA

(GENESIS 1—11)

 FAR FROM THE LAND OF EVERYDAY, OUT IN THE DISTANT curves OF the universe, lay strange and fantastic realms, unlike anything in our wildest dreams. Hidden by the barriers of time and space, they have lived forever beyond the reach of man, unknown and unexplored.

But now, just now, the cosmic veils have begun to lift a little. Man has had his first glimpses of these once-secret domains, and their bizarre ways have left him stunned. They challenge his very notions of matter and energy. Along with Alice in Wonderland, he says, "One can't believe impossible things."

And impossible, indeed, they seem to be. In those far reaches of the universe, in those bewildering worlds, are far places . . .

where a teaspoon of matter weighs as much as two hundred million elephants . . .

where a tiny whirling star winks on and off thirty times a second . . .

where a small, mysterious object shines with the brilliance of ten trillion suns . . .

where matter and light are continually sucked up by devouring black holes, never to be seen again.

Small wonder that the late British scientist J. B. S. Haldane could say, "The universe is not only queerer than we suppose, but queerer than we can suppose."

We used to think that the universe was simply our Milky Way Galaxy. Today we know that galaxies are as common as blades of grass in a meadow. They number perhaps a hundred billion.

How does one comprehend the incredible size of this galaxy-filled universe? For such awesome distances, scientists and astronomers think in terms of time, and they use the telescope as a time machine. They measure space by a unit called the light-year, the distance light travels in one year at the rate of 186,282 miles per second—about six trillion miles. (From *National Geographic*, May 1974.)

If you could shoot a gun whose bullet would travel around the world at the speed of light, the bullet would go around the world and pass through you seven times in one second!

Perhaps more than anything else, the mystery and the immensity of our universe capture our imagination and incite in us a fascination about the subject of Creation. There are countless unknowns and just as many "unbelievables." As we begin to explore the Creation Era, we will adopt a pattern that will be followed throughout the remainder of this section:

I.   You will review the main era, central figure, and main location you learned in the last chapter.

II.   You will read a brief story line summary of the events of that era, built around the central figure, with a three-word theme of each summary appearing in italics. Then you will be asked to review those three words to fill in the blanks.

III.   You will read an expansion of the summary of the events of that era.

I. **Review:** Fill in the blanks for this era.

STORY OF THE OLD TESTAMENT

ERA	FIGURE	LOCATION	STORY LINE SUMMARY
Creation	Adam	Eden	To be completed in this chapter

II. **Story Line Summary:** Adam is created by God, but he *sins* and *destroys* God's original *plan* for man.

ERA	SUMMARY
Creation	Adam is created by God, but he _sins_ and _destroys_ God's original _plan_ for man.

III. Expansion: There are four major events within the Creation Era. They are the accounts of:

1. Creation
2. Fall
3. Flood
4. Tower of Babel

1. Creation: Man created in the image of God (Genesis 1—2)

After a dramatic display of power in creating the heavens and the earth, God creates man. Adam and Eve are created in the image of God, in perfect fellowship and harmony with Him. Living in an idyllic setting in the Garden of Eden, they are individuals of beauty and high intelligence. The "image" is not a physical likeness, but a personal and spiritual likeness. Man has intellect, emotion, and will. He has a moral sense of right and wrong. He is a creative being. These are some characteristics of God that are shared by man, and in this sense, *man is created in the image of God*.

2. Fall: Sin entered the world (Genesis 3)

Satan, appearing in the form of a serpent, lures Adam and Eve into rebelling against God and violating the one prohibition God had given them: not to eat from the Tree of the Knowledge of Good and Evil. As a consequence, they are driven out of the Garden of Eden, and a curse is placed on the earth. When Adam and Eve rebel, *sin enters the world*. All the pain, all the evil, all the suffering endured by mankind for all time can be traced to that one act, which is, therefore, appropriately called the "Fall" of man.

3. Flood: Judgment for sin (Genesis 6—10)

Over the next several hundred years, as man multiplies in numbers, so his tendency to sin multiplies, until a time comes when God can find only eight people who are willing to live in a righteous relationship with Him: Noah, his wife, his three sons, and their wives.

So, in *judgment for sin*, God performs surgery on the human race, cutting out the cancerous tissue, as it were, and leaving behind the healthy tissue to restore itself. He does this by sending a worldwide flood which destroys mankind, except for Noah and his family, who are saved in Noah's ark.

4. **Tower: Beginning of the nations** (Genesis 11).

God's post-flood mandate to man was to spread out, populate, and subdue the whole earth. In direct disobedience to that command, man stays in one place and begins building a monument to himself, the Tower of Babel. God causes this large congregation of people to begin speaking different languages. Lack of communication prevents them from further progress on the tower, and the people of each tongue disperse to the four corners of the earth and form the *beginning of the nations* of the world as we know them today.

SELF-TEST

A. The Four Main Events of the Creation Era
(Write in the correct event from the options at left.)

OPTIONS:	EVENT:	DESCRIPTION:
Creation	*Flood*	Judgment for sin
Fall	*Tower*	Beginning of the nations
Flood	*Fall*	Sin entered the world
Tower	*Creation*	Man in the image of God

B. Story Line Summary
(Fill in the blanks from memory.)

ERA	SUMMARY
Creation	Adam is created by God, but he *sins* and *destroyed* God's original *plan* for man.

C. Arc of Bible History

(Fill in the name of the era. To check your answer, see the Appendix.)

1.	5.	9.
c reation		
2.	6.	10.
3.	7.	11.
4.	8.	12.

D. The Geography of the Creation Era

(Circle the dot indicating the possible location of Eden.)

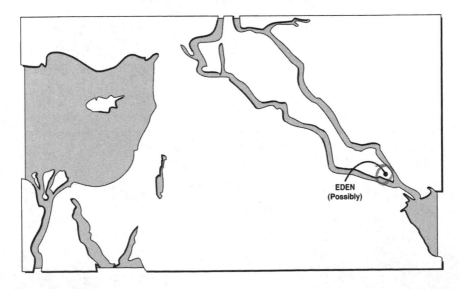

EDEN
(Possibly)

45

E. Story of the Old Testament

(Fill in the blanks.)

ERA	SUMMARY
Creation	Adam is created by God, but he _SINS_ and _destroys_ God's original _plan_ for man.

CHAPTER FIVE

THE PATRIARCH ERA

(GENESIS 12—50)

ANY PARENT WILL ADMIT THAT CONTROLLING CHILDREN IS A difficult and uncertain task.

In *I Want to Enjoy My Children*, psychologist Henry Brandt tells the story of the time he and his wife invited the president of the college he was attending to their house for dinner. They were nervous and had spent considerable time preparing the house and meal for a good impression. When the president arrived, they stumbled over themselves to make him comfortable. They sat him next to their two-year-old daughter for the meal. That was a mistake. During the meal, this little tot said to the president in her bird-like voice: "Please pass the salt." No one paid attention; they were listening to the president. So she tried again: "Will you please pass the salt?" Her small voice was easy to ignore as the adults strained for the president's every word. Finally, she hammered the distinguished guest on the arm and yelled, "Pass the salt, or I'll knock your block off!"

Even a president of the United States was perplexed by the antics of his child. Alice Roosevelt, daughter of Theodore Roosevelt, was an unruly girl whose antics scandalized the staid Washington "society" during her father's tenure at the White House. When a visitor objected to the girl's wandering in and out of the president's office while he was conducting important business with her father, Roosevelt said, "I can be president of the United States, or I can control Alice. I cannot possibly do both."

The Patriarch Era was a time of godly men presiding over a growing family. Abraham, Isaac, Jacob, and Joseph, successive generations of the same family, ruled over the Hebrew people in the earliest days of their existence.

On more than one occasion, Abraham must have felt a little like Brandt and Roosevelt. His descendants did not behave the way he wanted them to. Passion for God and what He wanted to do in and through the Hebrew people burned like a flame in Abraham's heart. But the flame dimmed in successive generations. However, the time of slavery in Egypt sharpened the spiritual hunger of the Hebrew people, and a great family, which became a great nation, emerged.

I. **Review:** Fill in the blanks to bring the chart up-to-date with this era.

STORY OF THE OLD TESTAMENT

ERA	FIGURE	LOCATION	STORY LINE SUMMARY
Creation	Adam	Eden	Adam is created by God, but he _SiNS_ and _destroys_ God's original _plan_ for man.
Patriarch	Abraham	Canaan	To be completed in this chapter.

II. **Story Line Summary:** *Abraham* is *chosen* by God to "father" a *people* to *represent* God to the world.

ERA	SUMMARY
Patriarch	*Abraham* is _Chosen_ by God to "father" a _people_ to _represent_ God to the world.

III. **Expansion:** There are four major men in the Patriarch Era:

1. Abraham
2. Isaac
3. Jacob
4. Joseph

1. Abraham: Father of the Hebrew people (Genesis 12—23)

Because of Adam's sin and the Fall of man, God's attention is now focused on a plan of redemption for mankind. God wants a people through whom He can work to produce a reflection of Himself, and through whom He can spread the message of redemption to the world. He chooses Abraham, who becomes the *father of the Hebrew people*, and promises him a country (land), countless descendants (seed), and a worldwide and timeless impact (blessing). Abraham is living in Ur, near the convergence of the Tigris and Euphrates Rivers, at the time. God leads him to the land of Canaan, where Abraham settles and has two sons, Ishmael and Isaac.

2. Isaac: Second father of promise (Genesis 24—26)

Isaac becomes the *second father of promise* as the fulfillment of Abraham's promises is passed down to him. He witnesses several major miracles during his life. He lives in the land of Abraham, becomes prosperous, and dies at an old age after having fathered two sons, Esau and Jacob.

3. Jacob: Father of the nation of Israel (Genesis 27—35)

The promises given to Abraham are passed through Isaac to Jacob, Isaac's younger son. Jacob begins life as a conniving scoundrel. However, through a series of miracles and other encounters with God, he mends his ways. Jacob has twelve sons, and the promises of Abraham are passed down to them all as a family. While Abraham is the father of the Hebrew people, Jacob is the *father of the nation of Israel*, as from his twelve sons emerge the twelve tribes of the nation of Israel.

4. Joseph: Leader in Egypt (Genesis 37—50)

Jacob's sons, for the most part, have very little commitment to God's call on them as a nation. They sell their brother Joseph as a slave, and he is taken to Egypt. Because of Joseph's righteousness, he rises to become a great *leader in Egypt*. During a severe famine, his family comes to Egypt for food, is reunited with Joseph, and as a result, enjoys peace and comfort. After Joseph dies, however, his people are enslaved for the next four hundred years. This time of trial sharpens the spiritual hunger of the Hebrew people, and they cry out to God for deliverance.

SELF-TEST

A. Major Men of the Patriarch Era

(Write in the correct name from the options at left.)

OPTIONS:	NAME:	DESCRIPTION:
Abraham	*Jacob*	Father of nation of Israel
Isaac	*Joseph*	Leader in Egypt
Jacob	*Abraham*	Father of Hebrew people
Joseph	*Isaac*	Second father of promise

B. Story Line Summary

(Fill in the blanks from memory.)

ERA	SUMMARY
Patriarch	Abraham is *chosen* by God to "father" a *people* to *represent* God to the world.

C. Arc of Bible History

(Fill in the names of the eras. To check your answers see the Appendix.)

1. *Creation*	5. *Judges*	9. *Silence*
2. *Patriarch*	6. *Kingdom*	10. *Gospels*
3. *Exodus*	7. *Exile*	11. *Church*
4. *Conquest*	8. *Return*	12. *Missions*

D. The Geography of the Patriarch Era

(Draw an arrow from Ur, where Abraham lived, to Canaan, and from Canaan to Egypt, to represent the geographical movements of the Patriarch Era.)

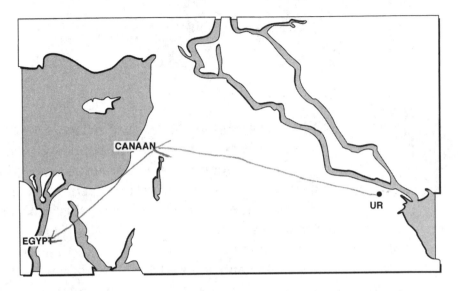

E. Story of the Old Testament

(Fill in the blanks.)

ERA	FIGURE	LOCATION	STORY LINE SUMMARY
Creation	Adam	Eden	Adam is created by God, but he _si'ns_ and _destroys_ God's original _plan_ for man.
Patriarch	Abraham	Canaan	*Abraham is* _chosen_ by God to "father" a _people_ to _represent_ God to the world.

CHAPTER SIX

THE EXODUS ERA

(EXODUS—DEUTERONOMY)

 THE EXODUS WAS THE MASS MOVEMENT OF THE ISRAELITES OUT of slavery in Egypt back to the Promised Land in Canaan. It was not an easy movement. The Pharaoh of Egypt did not want them to go, and he threatened them with military retaliation. The miracles God performed during this time are among the most spectacular recorded in the Bible—the Nile River turned to blood, shepherds' rods turned into snakes, the firstborn of every Egyptian household died, and the Red Sea parted to allow the Israelites to cross over on dry land, escaping the Egyptian army.

Movies have sometimes portrayed this event as a little band of nomads roaming about the desert, camping under palm trees and singing Hebrew folk songs around a small campfire. This picture could hardly be further from the truth. The Book of Numbers tells us that when the Israelites left Egypt, there were six hundred thousand fighting men. It is reasonable to assume that if there were six hundred thousand fighting men, there were also six hundred thousand women. That's 1,200,000. Each of those families may have had at least two children. That's another 1,200,000. In addition there were the men who were too old to fight, and their wives. There was the priestly tribe, the Levites, who didn't fight, and their wives and their children. There were, conservatively speaking, between two and a half to three million people who left Egypt during this "Exodus."

This was not a little tribe of nomads roaming about the desert. This was a nation on the move. Look at the state of Texas on a map and imagine the city of Dallas beginning to move across the map, and you get an idea of the magnitude of the Exodus. When you add all the animals they took with them for food and milk, as well as for sacrifices, this qualified as a horde! Instead of looking for a flat spot under a palm tree to camp, they had to look for a valley ten miles square. When they lined up to cross the Red Sea, it was more than a little aisle that was required. If they crossed the Red Sea one hundred abreast, counting the animals, the column would have stretched perhaps as far as fifty miles back into the desert.

Personal beliefs aside, this ranks as one of the greatest historical events of the ancient world, and this was an event over which Moses presided. To get a better look at the specifics of the Exodus, we will now review our previous chapters and then look at the four main events of the Exodus Era.

I. Review: Fill in the blanks to bring the chart up-to-date with this era. To check your answers see the Appendix.

STORY OF THE OLD TESTAMENT

ERA	FIGURE	LOCATION	STORY LINE SUMMARY
Creation	Adam	Eden	Adam is created by God, but he _Sins_ and _destroys_ God's original _plan_ for man.
Patriarch	Abraham	Canaan	Abraham is _Chosen_ by God to "father" a _people_ to _represent_ God to the world.
Exodus	Moses	Egypt	To be completed in this chapter

II. Story Line Summary: Through Moses God *delivers* the Hebrew people from *slavery* in Egypt and then gives them the *Law*.

ERA	SUMMARY
Exodus	Through Moses God _delivers_ the Hebrew people from _slavery_ in Egypt and then gives them the _Law_.

III. Expansion: There are four major events in the Exodus Era:

1. Deliverance
2. The Law
3. Kadesh Barnea
4. Forty Years of Wandering

1. Deliverance: Freedom from slavery in Egypt
   (Exodus 1—18)
   The Hebrews have languished under slavery in Egypt for four hundred years when they cry out to God for deliverance. God raises up Moses as His spokesman to Pharaoh, the ruler of Egypt, asking for spiritual freedom for the Hebrew people. Pharaoh refuses, and a series of ten plagues is levied on Egypt to prompt Pharaoh to let the people go. The plagues start out bad and they get worse— from frogs, to gnats, to water turned to blood, to the death of the firstborn in every household of Egypt. Finally, Pharaoh consents to let the Hebrews leave Egypt. After they have gone, he changes his mind and attempts to recapture them. They are as far as the Red Sea when God parts the Red Sea and the Hebrew people cross over to the other side. The waters come together again, protecting them from the Egyptian army and *freeing them from slavery in Egypt*. God, of course, has only one destination for them: the Promised Land of Canaan. . . the land "flowing with milk and honey." The land that their father Abraham had first settled is again to be their home.

2. The Law: God's commandments at Mount Sinai
   (Exodus 19—40)
   The Hebrew people now begin to take on a national identity as Israel. From the Red Sea, the Israelites travel south to the bottom of

the Sinai Peninsula and camp at Mount Sinai. They receive *God's commandments at Mount Sinai*. Moses meets with God alone at the top of Mount Sinai, where he receives the Ten Commandments written on tablets of stone by the finger of God. Moses also receives a full revelation of the Law that is to govern Israel's national life as well as her relationship to God. God promises to bless her abundantly for obedience and curse her soundly for disobedience.

3. **Kadesh Barnea: Place of rebellion against God**
   (Numbers 10—14)
   Israel leaves Mount Sinai and migrates north to an oasis, Kadesh Barnea, which is the southern gateway into the Promised Land. From this vantage point, twelve spies are sent into the Promised Land, one spy from each of the twelve tribes of Israel. The land is inhabited by the Canaanites, who would not take kindly to an Israelite horde coming back into the land. When the spies return, they have some good news and some bad news. The good news is that the land *is* beautiful and bountiful, "flowing with milk and honey." The bad news is that there are giants and hostile armies throughout the land. Ten spies report that the land is indomitable (in spite of the fact that God has promised to give them victory over any opposing forces). Two spies, Joshua and Caleb, exhort the people to believe God and go into the land. The people believe the majority report and refuse to follow Moses into the land. Thus, this becomes known as *a place of rebellion against God*.

4. **Forty Years of Wandering: Consequences of rebelling against God** (Numbers 20—36)
   As a *consequence of rebelling against God* at Kadesh Barnea, the "Exodus" generation is condemned to wander in the wilderness until everyone who was twenty-one years old or older at the time dies. In the ensuing forty years, a new generation comes to leadership; it is willing to follow the leaders into the land. Moses leads them to the north of the Dead Sea near Jericho, the eastern gateway to the Promised Land. Moses encourages the people, gives them additional instruction found in the Book of Deuteronomy, and then dies.

SELF-TEST

A. Four Major Events in the Exodus Era
(Write in the correct name from the options at left.)

OPTIONS:	EVENT:	DESCRIPTION:
Deliverance	*The Law*	God's commandments at Mount Sinai
The Law	*Kadesh Barnea*	Place of rebellion against God
Kadesh Barnea	*Forty Years of Wandering*	Consequences of rebelling against God
Forty Years of Wandering	*Deliverance*	Freedom from slavery in Egypt

B. Story Line Summary:
Through Moses God *delivers* the Hebrew people from *slavery* in Egypt and then gives them the *Law*.

ERA	SUMMARY
Exodus	Through Moses God *delivers* the Hebrew people from *slavery* in Egypt and then gives them the *Law*.

C. Arc of Bible History
(Fill in the names of the eras.)

1. Creation	5.	9.
2. Patriarch	6.	10.
3. E Exodus	7.	11.
4.	8.	12.

D. The Geography of the Exodus Era
(Draw an arrow from Egypt through the Red Sea to Mount Sinai to Kadesh Barnea, and then to the top of the Dead Sea on the east side of the Jordan River. This represents the geographical movement of the Exodus Era.)

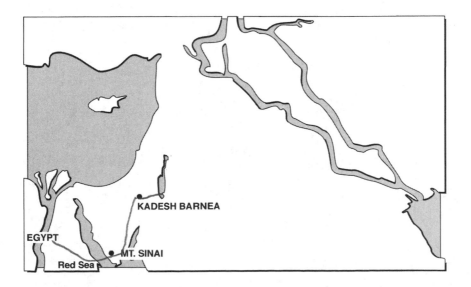

E. Story of the Old Testament

(Fill in the blanks. To check your answers, see the Appendix.)

ERA	FIGURE	LOCATION	STORY LINE SUMMARY
Creation	Adam	Eden	Adam is created by God, but he _sins_ and _destroys_ God's original _plan_ for man.
Patriarch	Abraham	Canaan	*Abraham is* _chosen_ by God to "father" a _people_ to _represent_ God to the world.
Exodus	Moses	Egypt	Through Moses God _delivers_ the Hebrew people from _slavery_ in Egypt and then gives them the _Law_.

CHAPTER SEVEN

THE CONQUEST ERA

(JOSHUA)

THE DAYS WERE DARK INDEED FOR GREAT BRITAIN IN 1940. The British people were at war with Germany and were being pressed hard on every side by the Nazi military machine. Supplies and morale were low. Their national destiny hung in the balance. Then a new prime minister came on the scene: Winston Churchill. He was a man of intense conviction, deep resolve, and unquenchable optimism. His speeches in the first months of his term burst upon the world with sudden and magnificent power. From them we read:

To form an administration of this scale and complexity is a serious undertaking in itself, but it must be remembered that we are in the preliminary stage of one of the greatest battles in history, that we are in action at many points in Norway and in Holland, that we have to be prepared in the Mediterranean, that the air battle is continuous, and that many preparations have to be made here at home. I would say to the House, as I said to those who have joined this Government: I have nothing to offer but blood, toil, tears, and sweat.

You ask what is our policy? I will say: It is to wage war by sea, land, and air with all our might and with all the strength that God can give us: to wage war against a monstrous tyranny, never surpassed in the dark, lamentable catalogue of human crime. That is our policy. You ask, what is our aim? I can answer in a word: Victory—victory at all costs, victory in spite of all the terror, victory however long and hard the road may be; for without victory, there is no survival.

I have, myself, full confidence that if all do their duty, if nothing is neglected, and if the best arrangements are made, as they are being made, we shall prove ourselves once again able to defend our island home . . . to ride out the storm of war, and to outlive the menace of tyranny. Even though large tracts of Europe and many old and famous states have fallen or may fall into the grip of the Gestapo and all the odious apparatus of Nazi rule, we shall not flag or fail. We shall go on to the end, we shall fight in France, we shall fight on the seas and oceans, we shall fight with growing confidence and grow-ing strength in the air, we shall defend our island, whatever the cost may be, we shall fight on the beaches, we shall fight on the landing grounds, we shall fight in the fields and in the streets, we shall fight in the hills; we shall never surrender.

After the Exodus, the circumstances were also perilous for the Israelites. They had wandered in the wilderness for forty years because of rebellion and unbelief at Kadesh Barnea. Now they were at Jericho, and the test was the same. Would they resolve to forge ahead, or would they shrink from the circumstances as their fathers had done?

The task of rallying and leading the people fell to Joshua. Moses, the great leader of the last forty years, was dead. Would the people galvanize behind Joshua? Or would they refuse his leadership? Just as England faced a crossroads when Churchill became its leader, so also the Israelites faced a critical fork in the road.

I. **Review:** Fill in the blanks to bring the chart up-to-date with this era.

STORY OF THE OLD TESTAMENT

ERA	FIGURE	LOCATION	STORY LINE SUMMARY
Creation	Adam	Eden	Adam is created by God, but he _sins_ and _destroys_ God's original _plan_ for man.
Patriarch	abraham	Canaan	*Abraham* is ___chosen___ by God to "father" a ___people___ to ___represent___ God to the world.

ERA	FIGURE	LOCATION	STORY LINE SUMMARY
Exodus	*Moses*	*Egypt*	Through Moses God _delivers_ the Hebrew people from _slavery_ in Egypt and then gives them the _Law_ .
Conquest	*Joshua*	*Canaan*	To be completed in this chapter.

II. Story Line Summary: *Joshua* leads the *conquest* of the *Promised Land.*

ERA	SUMMARY
Conquest	Joshua leads the _conquest_ of the _Promised Land_ .

III. Expansion: There are four main events in the Conquest Era:
1. Jordan
2. Jericho
3. Conquest
4. Dominion

1. Jordan: A miraculous parting of water (Joshua 1—5)

Moses dies, and God hand-picks Joshua to succeed him. Joshua's first challenge is to cross the Jordan River at flood stage. God commands him to prepare the nation for a ceremonial procession and to begin walking, priests first, toward the Jordan River. When the priests touched water, God would part the water for them. (This is the second *miraculous "parting of water"* that God performed for Israel. The first was the parting of the Red Sea.) The people respond, and God parts the Jordan River for a distance of about twenty miles. They cross without incident, and the water begins flowing again.

2 Jericho: A miraculous conquest of a city (Joshua 6)

The city of Jericho, a small oasis on the west side of the Jordan River near the Dead Sea, is not only the eastern gateway to the

Promised Land, but it is also a fortified city and poses a threat to the welfare of Israel. Joshua is a brilliant military strategist, so much so that his campaigns in the Bible are still studied in the Army War College today. As he stands overlooking the city, contemplating how to conquer it, the angel of the Lord appears to him and instructs him to march around the city once a day for seven days. On the seventh day, he is to march around it seven times and the people are to shout. The city wall will fall down. They did, and it did . . . *a miraculous conquest of a city!*

3. Conquest: The defeat of Canaan (Joshua 7—12)

The Canaanites are united in their hatred of the Israelites, but not in their military opposition to them. Primarily, the region is characterized by individual kings, each with his own city and surrounding country. Joshua cuts through the midsection toward the Mediterranean Sea. Having divided the land, he then begins to conquer, from South to North. In about seven years the initial *defeat of Canaan* is complete.

4. Dominion: Finalizing dominion (Joshua 13—20)

Each of the twelve tribes of Israel is given a land area by lottery and is responsible for *finalizing dominion* over that area. All twelve tribes inhabit their areas and form a loose federation with the other tribes.

SELF-TEST

A. Four Major Events in the Conquest Era
(Write in the correct event from the options at left.)

OPTIONS:	EVENT:	DESCRIPTION:
Jordan	*Conquest*	The defeat of Canaan
Jericho	*Jordan*	A miraculous parting of water
Conquest	*Dominion*	Finalizing dominion
Dominion	*Jericho*	A miraculous conquest of a city

B. Story Line Summary

(Fill in the blanks from memory.)

ERA	SUMMARY
Conquest	Joshua leads the *Conquest* of the *Promised Land*.

C. Arc of Bible History

(Fill in the names of the eras. To check your answers, see the Appendix.)

1. Creation	5.	9.
2. Patriarch	6.	10.
3. Exodus	7.	11.
4. Conquest	8.	12.

D. The Geography of the Conquest Era

(Draw an arrow from Jericho across to the Mediterranean Sea. Then draw an arrow into the southern half of the land. Now draw an arrow into the northern half of the land. This represents the geographical movement of the Conquest Era.)

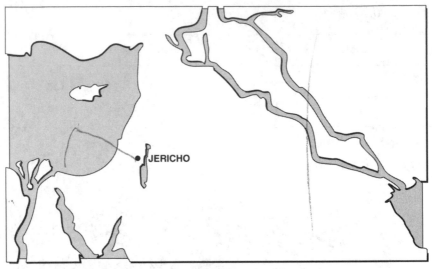

JERICHO

E. Story of the Old Testament *(Fill in the blanks.)*

ERA	FIGURE	LOCATION	STORY LINE SUMMARY
Creation	Adam	Eden	Adam is created by God, but he _Sins_ and _destroys_ God's original _plan_ for man.
Patriarch	Abraham	Canaan	*Abraham* is _chosen_ by God to "father" a _people_ to _represent_ God to the world.
Exodus	Moses	Egypt	Through Moses God _delivers_ the Hebrew people from _slavery_ in Egypt and then gives them the _Law_.
Conquest	Joshua	Canaan	*Joshua* leads the _Conquest_ of the _Promised Land_.

CHAPTER EIGHT

THE JUDGES ERA

(JUDGES—RUTH)

WOMAN IN RAGS, GARBAGE, REVEALED AS HEIRESS

SO READ THE HEADLINE IN THE *SAN FRANCISCO CHRONICLE* concerning a lady known as "Garbage Mary" who was picked up in a shopping mall in Delray Beach, Florida. She appeared to be just another derelict whose mind had faded. Neighbors told stories of her scrounging through garbage cans for food, which she hoarded in her car and her two-room apartment. There were mounds of garbage in the small apartment, stuffed in the refrigerator, the stove, the sink, the cabinets, and the bathtub. There were paths through the garbage. Other than in the kitchen, there were no chairs to sit in because they were piled with trash.

Police finally identified her as the daughter of a well-to-do lawyer and bank director from Illinois who had died several years earlier. In addition to the garbage, police found Mobil Oil stock worth more than four hundred thousand dollars, documents indicating ownership of oil fields in Kansas, stock certificates from firms such as U.S. Steel, Uniroyal, and Squibb, and passbooks for eight large bank accounts.

Garbage Mary was a millionaire who was living like a derelict. Untold wealth was at her disposal, and yet she scrounged through garbage rather than claim the resources that were rightly hers.

The parallel between Garbage Mary and Israel during the time of the judges is striking. This was a dark period indeed in the history of the Jewish people. They had lost their spiritual moorings, and, as is recorded in the final verse of the Book of Judges, "everyone did what was right in his own eyes." The result was a morally degraded, socially perverted, and spiritually bankrupt time of almost four hundred years. Israel had all the wealth of the promises of God at their disposal. Yet they scavenged through the garbage of life, eking out a pitiful existence. They could have been kings but lived like paupers.

I. Review: Fill in the blanks to bring the chart up-to-date with this era.

STORY OF THE OLD TESTAMENT

ERA	FIGURE	LOCATION	STORY LINE SUMMARY
Creation	Adam	Eden	Adam is created by God, but he _sins_ and _destroys_ God's original _plan_ for man.
Patriarch	Abraham	Canaan	*Abraham* is _chosen_ by God to "father" a _people_ to _represent_ God to the world.
Exile	Moses	Egypt	Through Moses God _delivers_ the Hebrew people from _slavery_ in Egypt and then gives them the _Law_.
Conquest	Joshua	Canaan	*Joshua* leads the _conquest_ of the _Promised_ _Land_.
Judges	Samson	Canaan	To be completed in this chapter.

II. Story Line Summary: *Samson* and others were chosen as *judges* to *govern* the people for *four hundred* rebellious years.

ERA	SUMMARY
Judges	*Samson* and others were chosen as *judges* to *govern* the people for *four* *hundred* rebellious years.

III. Expansion: There are four main subjects in the Judges Era:

1. Judges
2. Rebellion
3. Cycles
4. Ruth

1. Judges: The leaders of Israel (Judges)

As seen in the Book of Judges, these judges are not men who wear long, flowing black robes, sit on high benches, and make legal decisions. Rather, they are political-military *leaders of Israel* who exercise nearly absolute power because of their office and abilities. The four major judges are:

- Deborah, a woman judge early in the Judges Era
- Gideon, who defeats an army of thousands with only three hundred men
- Samson, the most famous judge, whose fabulous strength has captured our imagination for thousands of years
- Samuel, a transitional character held in very high regard in Scripture, who is both the last judge and the first prophet

2. Rebellion: The breaking of God's Law (Judges)

The Book of Judges records the darkest period in Israel's history, following one of the brightest eras: the Conquest Era under Joshua. Just before Moses dies, he instructs Israel (in Deuteronomy 7:1–5) to do three things:

1. Destroy all the inhabitants of Canaan.
2. Avoid intermarriage with the Canaanites.
3. Shun worship of the Canaanite gods.

Israel fails on all three accounts. *The breaking of God's Law* and the record of Israel's subsequent moral degradation are sad indeed.

3. Cycles: Repetition of Israel's misfortunes (Judges)

Much of the Era of Judges involves a series of seven cycles that are recorded in the Book of Judges. Each cycle has five component parts: (1) Israel "sins," (2) God disciplines them through military "conquest" by a neighboring country, (3) Israel "repents" and cries out to God for deliverance, (4) God raises up a judge who "delivers" them from bondage, and (5) God "frees" the land from military oppression for the remainder of that judge's life. That is one cycle: sin, conquest, repentance, deliverance, and freedom. Then, when a judge dies, the *repetition of Israel's misfortunes* begins again. The Israelites fall into sin again, followed by conquest, followed by repentance, etc. Seven such cycles are recorded in the Book of Judges.

4. Ruth: A model woman (Ruth)

Standing out in refreshing contrast to the general background of the Judges Era is Ruth, described in the book that bears her name. This *model woman* who lives during the Era of Judges is an example of moral and spiritual strength. Her story is one of love, purity, and commitment. She is a living illustration of the blessings that God showers on those who live in faithful obedience to Him. One example of God's blessings toward Ruth is that she, a non-Hebrew, is listed in the lineage from Abraham to Jesus.

SELF-TEST

A. Four Major Subjects in the Judges Era

(Write in the correct subject from the options at left.)

OPTIONS:	SUBJECT:	DESCRIPTION:
Judges	*Ruth*	A model woman
Rebellion	*Judges*	The leaders of Israel
Cycles	*Rebellion*	The breaking of God's Law
Ruth	*Cycles*	Repetition of Israel's misfortunes

B. Story Line Summary
(Fill in the blanks from memory.)

ERA	SUMMARY
Judges	*Samson* and others were chosen as ___judges___ to ___govern___ the people for ___four___ ___hundred___ rebellious years.

C. Arc of Bible History
(Fill in the names of the eras. To check your answers, see the Appendix.)

1. Creation	5. Judges	9. Silence
2. Patriarch	6. Kingdom	10. Gospels
3. Exodus	7. Exile	11. Church
4. Conquest	8. Return	12. Missions

D. The Geography of the Judges Era
(Match the numbers below with the blanks on the map to see the countries conquering Israel in the Judges Era.)

1. Philistia
2. Moab
3. Mesopotamia
4. Canaan
5. Ammon
6. Midian

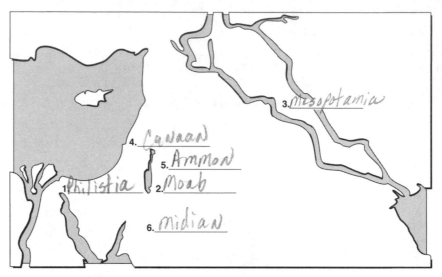

On the map (handwritten labels):
- 3. Mesopotamia
- 4. Canaan
- 5. Ammon
- 1. Philistia
- 2. Moab
- 6. Midian

E. Story of the Old Testament *(Fill in the blanks.)*

ERA	FIGURE		STORY LINE SUMMARY
Creation	Adam	Eden	Adam is created by God, but he _sins_ and _destroys_ God's original _plan_ for man.
Patriarch	Abraham	Canaan	*Abraham* is _chosen_ by God to "father" a _people_ to _represent_ God to the world.
Exodus	Moses	Egypt	Through Moses God _delivers_ the Hebrew people from _slavery_ in Egypt and then gives them the _LAW_.
Conquest	Joshua	Canaan	*Joshua* leads the _conquest_ of the _Promised_ _LAND_.
Judges	Samson	Canaan	*Samson* and others were chosen as _judges_ to _govern_ the people for _four hundred_ rebellious years.

CHAPTER NINE

THE KINGDOM ERA

(1 SAMUEL—2 CHRONICLES)

IF YOU WOULD BE FREE TO SAIL THE SEVEN SEAS, YOU MUST make yourself a slave to the compass. By nature, man desires something he cannot have: total freedom. There are certain freedoms we can have, but they have corresponding bondages. And there are certain bondages we can have that afford us corresponding freedoms. For example, you can be free from the toothbrush and in bondage to cavities, or you can make yourself a slave to the toothbrush and be free from cavities. You cannot be free from the toothbrush *and* free from cavities. That kind of freedom, total freedom, does not exist.

Throughout life, we are constantly making choices, and for those choices, we pay certain inescapable consequences. Freedom comes with a price.

The kings of Israel wanted total freedom. They wanted the freedom to ignore the directives God had given them on how to rule and wage war. But at the same time, they wanted the freedom to have economic and military prosperity. This was not possible. As a result, the Kingdom Era was a very turbulent time with many ups and downs. When a righteous king ruled, the nation would prosper. When an unrighteous king gained the throne, the nation would falter.

The barnacles of unrighteousness began to affix themselves to the Israeli ship of state, and before the books of history were completed, the nation had collapsed and suffered at the hands of warring neighbors.

I. Review: Fill in the blanks to bring the chart up-to-date with this era. To check your answers, see the Appendix.

STORY OF THE OLD TESTAMENT

ERA	FIGURE		STORY LINE SUMMARY
Creation	Adam	Eden	Adam is created by God, but he _sins_ and _destroys_ God's original _plan_ for man.
Patriarch	Abraham	Canaan	Abraham is _chosen_ by God to "father" a _people_ to _represent_ God to the world.
Exodus	Moses	Egypt	Through Moses God _delivers_ the Hebrew people from _slavery_ in Egypt and then gives them the _LAW_.
Conquest	Joshua	Canaan	Joshua leads the _conquest_ of the _Promised land_.
Judges	Samson	Canaan	Samson and others were chosen as _judges_ to _govern_ the people for _four hundred_ rebellious years.
Kingdom	David	Israel	To be completed in this chapter.

II. Story Line Summary: *David,* the greatest king in the new *monarchy,* is followed by a succession of mostly *unrighteous* kings, and God eventually *judges* Israel for her sin, sending her into exile.

ERA	SUMMARY
Kingdom	*David*, the greatest king in the new _monarchy_, is followed by a succession of mostly _unrighteous_ kings, and God eventually _judges_ Israel for her sin, sending her into exile.

III. **Expansion:** There are four main periods in the Kingdom Era:
1. United Kingdom
2. Division of the Kingdom
3. Northern Kingdom
4. Southern Kingdom

1. United Kingdom: A new monarchy (1 and 2 Samuel)

The twelve tribes of Israel, jealous of other nations around them, are united in their demand to God for a king. God allows Samuel, the last judge, to anoint Saul to be the first king, beginning *a new monarchy*. Because Saul is not a righteous king, God does not honor his reign or establish his family on the throne of Israel. His successor, David, though having shortcomings, is a righteous king, and Israel prospers under him. David's son Solomon becomes king upon David's death. Solomon rules righteously at first, then drifts from the Lord.

2. Divided Kingdom: A civil war (1 Kings)

As a result of Solomon's spiritual drifting, *a civil war* erupts upon his death, and the kingdom is divided. There is now a northern kingdom, consisting of ten tribes, and a southern kingdom, consisting of the tribes of Judah and Benjamin. The northern ten tribes retain the name "Israel," and the southern two tribes adopt the name "Judah," after the name of the larger tribe.

3. Northern Kingdom: The unrighteous kingdom (2 Kings)

In the civil war that splits the kingdom, Jeroboam commands the northern kingdom of Israel. He is unrighteous, and every other king (nineteen total) who succeeds him during the two-hundred-fifty-year life of the northern kingdom is also unrighteous. Because of this unrighteousness, God raises up Assyria to conquer the northern kingdom and scatter His people to the four winds. *The unrighteous kingdom* is never restored.

4. Southern Kingdom: The inconsistent kingdom (2 Kings)

Rehoboam, Solomon's son, commands the southern kingdom of Judah. He is also unrighteous, but the southern kingdom fares somewhat better than the northern. Lasting for four hundred years, its life is prolonged by eight righteous kings out of a total of twenty. Judah's sins finally catch up to her, however, and God brings judgment on *the inconsistent kingdom* by raising up Babylonia (which had conquered Assyria) to conquer Judah. Babylonia gathers all the leaders, artisans, musicians, and promising children, and takes them away to captivity in Babylonia.

SELF-TEST

A. Four Major Subjects in the Kingdom Era

(Write in the correct subject from the options at left.)

OPTIONS:	SUBJECT:	DESCRIPTION:
United Kingdom	*Northern Kingdom*	The unrighteous kingdom
Divided Kingdom	*United Kingdom*	A new monarchy
Northern Kingdom	*Southern Kingdom*	The inconsistent kingdom
Southern Kingdom	*Divided Kingdom*	A civil war

B. Story Line Summary

(Fill in the blanks from memory.)

ERA	SUMMARY
Kingdom	*David*, the greatest king in the new *monarchy*, is followed by a succession of mostly *unrighteous* kings, and God eventually *judges* Israel for her sin, sending her into exile.

C. Arc of Bible History

(Fill in the names of the eras. To check your answers, see the Appendix.)

1. Creation	5. Judges	9. Silence
2. Patriarch	6. Kingdoms	10. Gospels
3. Exidus	7. Exile	11. Church
4. Conquest	8. Return	12. Missions

D. The Geography of the Kingdom Era

(Draw an arrow from Israel to Assyria. Draw another arrow from Judah to Babylonia. This represents the geographical movement of the Kingdom Era.)

E. Story of the Old Testament

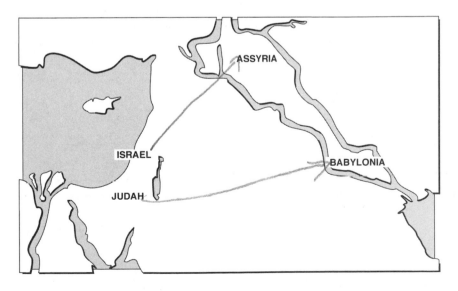

(Fill in the blanks.)

ERA	FIGURE		STORY LINE SUMMARY
Creation	Adam	Eden	Adam is created by God, but he _sins_ and _destroys_ God's original _plan_ for man.
Patriarch	Abraham	Canaan	*Abraham* is _chosen_ by God to "father" a _people_ to _represent_ God to the world.
Exodus	Moses	Egypt	Through Moses God _delivers_ the Hebrew people from _slavery_ in Egypt and then gives them the _Law_.
Conquest	Joshua	Canaan	*Joshua* leads the _conquest_ of the _Promised Land_.
Judges	Samson	Canaan	*Samson* and others were chosen as _judges_ to _govern_ the people for _4_ _hundred_ rebellious years.
Kingdom	David	Israel	*David*, the greatest king in the new _monarchy_, is followed by a succession of mostly _unrighteous_ kings, and God eventually _judges_ Israel for her sin, sending her into exile.

CHAPTER TEN

THE EXILE ERA

(EZEKIEL—DANIEL)

 IT IS ONE OF THE BASIC LAWS OF PHYSICS THAT THINGS TEND to run down or deteriorate. Deterioration in relationships can be illustrated in something as mundane as the common cold. An old edition of *The Saturday Evening Post* included this description of "The Seven Stages of the Married Cold":

Stage 1: Sugar dumpling, I'm really worried about my baby girl. That's a bad sniffle and there's no telling about these things with all the "strep" that's going around. I'm going to put you in the hospital for a general check-up and good rest. I know the food's terrible, but I'm going to bring you dinner every night from "Rosini's." I've got it all arranged with the floor supervisor.

Stage 2: Listen, darling, I don't like the sound of that cough. I'm going to call Doc Miller to rush over here. Now you go to bed like a good girl just for papa.

Stage 3: Maybe you'd better lie down, honey. Nothing like a little rest when you feel lousy. I'll bring you something. Have you got any canned soup?

Stage 4: Now look, dear, be sensible. After you've fed the kids and gotten the dishes done and the floor mopped, you'd better lie down.

Stage 5: Why don't you take a couple of aspirin?

Stage 6: If you'd just gargle something instead of sitting around barking like a seal all evening. . . .

Stage 7: Would you stop coughing on me?! Are you trying to give me pneumonia?!

We must recognize also that our actions have certain repercussions in our relationships.

A troubled man was standing at the top of the Empire State Building in New York and finally he decided to jump off, ending his own life. After he had fallen awhile and was only one hundred stories off the ground, he realized he had made a mistake. It was wrong to commit suicide, and he knew it. He said, "O God, if you hear me . . . I'm sorry for the foolish mistake I made in jumping off this building. I repent, and I would like to know if you would forgive me." A voice came back. "Of course I forgive you. Don't think a thing about it. I will never bring it up again. And by the way, I'll see you in just a minute."

Sin is a fact of human existence. And God will forgive whoever comes to Him in repentance. But that doesn't change the fact that sin has consequences. God forgives the man for jumping off the building, but the man will still fall to the ground.

Israel tasted this bitter reality. Their relationship with the Lord deteriorated. They lived in roller-coaster rebellion against Him for four hundred years during the Kingdom Era, continually paying the price. Finally, the debt became so great that judgment came in the form of military conquest. During the time of the Exile, there were some great spiritual leaders, and there was repentance on the part of a segment of the Jewish people. However, this did not remove the penalty for the years of rebellion, and the full price of the Exile was exacted.

I. Review: Fill in the blanks to bring the chart up-to-date with this era.

STORY OF THE OLD TESTAMENT

ERA	FIGURE		STORY LINE SUMMARY
Creation	_Adam_	_Eden_	Adam is created by God, but he _sins_ and _destroys_ God's original _plan_ for man.
Patriarch	_Abraham_	_Canaan_	Abraham is _chosen_ by God to "father" a _people_ to _represent_ God to the world.

ERA	FIGURE		STORY LINE SUMMARY
Exodus	*Moses*	*Egypt*	Through Moses God _delivers_ the Hebrew people from _slavery_ in Egypt and then gives them the _Law_ .
Conquest	*Joshua*	*Canaan*	*Joshua* leads the _conquest_ of the _Promised Land_.
Judges	*Samson*	*Canaan*	*Samson* and others were chosen as _judges_ to _govern_ the people for _400_ rebellious years.
Kingdoms	*David*	*Israel*	*David*, the greatest king in the new _monarchy_ is followed by a succession of mostly _unrighteous_ kings, and God eventually _judges_ Israel for her sin, sending her into exile.
Exile	*Daniel*	*Babylon*	To be completed in this chapter.

II. Story Line Summary: *Daniel* gives *leadership* and encourages *faithfulness* among the *exiles* for the next seventy years.

ERA	SUMMARY
Exile	*Daniel* gives _leadership_ and encourages _faithfulness_ among the _exiles_ for the next seventy years.

III. Expansion: As mentioned before in Chapter 1 of this book, some history is contained in books that are primarily Prophetical Books, and that is the case in the Exile Era. You will note that the biblical references for the four main divisions of this era will include some Prophetical Books. There are four main divisions in the Exile Era:

1. Prophecy
2. Prophets
3. Exiles
4. Power Change

1. Prophecy: Warning of impending captivity (Jeremiah)

The northern kingdom, Israel, has been conquered by Assyria and is dispersed in 722 B.C. During the time of the events described in 2 Kings, the southern kingdom, Judah, receives a *warning of impending captivity* through Jeremiah (called the "Weeping Prophet"), who prophesies that the nation will be taken into captivity at the hands of the Babylonians. This happens in 586 B.C. He also accurately prophesies that the captivity will last seventy years.

2. Prophets: Encouraging faithfulness of exiles
(Ezekiel and Daniel)

There are two prophets who write books of the Bible during the exile: Ezekiel and Daniel. Not a great deal is known about the prophet Ezekiel since his book is mostly prophetic and not autobiographical. He foretells of national restoration and *encourages faithfulness among the exiles*. Daniel's book, while a book of prophecy, is more biographical. He is a prominent governmental leader, much like Joseph in Egypt. While Daniel's personal life is an example to his people, his prophecies tend to concern the future destruction of the world.

3. Exiles: Assimilated into the culture (Daniel)

The Book of Daniel also gives us a glimpse of life among the exiles. Apparently, the Jews are *assimilated into the culture* in which they are exiled. They experience discrimination, which has always been true of displaced Jews. Yet, in spite of this, they seem fairly well integrated into society, and some of them achieve positions of prominence.

4. Power Change: Persian Empire expands (Daniel)

While the Jews are in exile in Babylonia, Persia rises to become the dominant military power of that region. Persia conquers Babylonia (which had conquered Assyria), so now Persia rules not only her own land, but the land once dominated by Assyria and Babylonia. The *Persian Empire expands* from the Tigris River to the Mediterranean Sea.

SELF-TEST

A. Four Major Subjects in the Exile Era

(Write in the correct subject from the options at left.)

OPTIONS:	SUBJECT:	DESCRIPTION:
Prophecy	*Power Change*	Persian empire expands
Prophets	*Exiles*	Assimilated into the culture
Exiles	*Prophecy*	Warning of impending captivity
Power Change	*Prophets*	Encouraging faithfulness of exile

B. Story Line Summary

(Fill in the blanks from memory.)

ERA	SUMMARY
Exile	*Daniel* gives *Leadership* and encourages *faithfulness* among the *exiles* for the next seventy years.

C. Arc of Bible History

(Fill in the names of the eras.)

1. *Adam* *Canaan* Creation	5. *Samson* Judges	9. *Silence* *changes* *Jerusalem*
2. *Abraham* *Canaan* Patriarch	6. *David* *Israel* Kingdom	10. *Gospels* *Jesus* *Palestine*
3. *Moses* *Egypt* Exodus	7. *Daniel* *Babylonia* Exiles	11. *Church* *Peter* *Jerusalem*
4. *Joshua* *Canaan* Conquest	8. *Return* *Ezra* *Jerusalem*	12. *Missions* *Paul* *Roman Empire*

D. The Geography of the Exile Era

(Draw a line from Babylonia toward Assyria and circle Assyria. Draw another line from Persia toward Babylonia, encircling both Babylonia and Assyria. This represents the shift in power during the Exile Era. Assyria had conquered Israel. Then Babylonia conquered Assyria and Judah. Finally, Persia conquered Babylonia and ended up ruling everyone.)

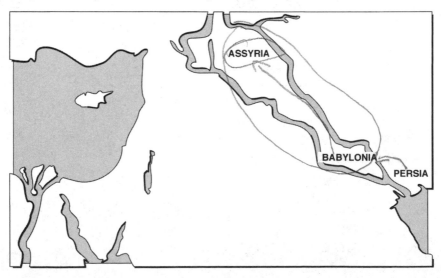

E. Story of the Old Testament

(Fill in the blanks. To check your answer, see the Appendix.)

ERA	FIGURE		STORY LINE SUMMARY
Creation	Adam	Eden	Adam is created by God, but he _sins_ and _destroys_ God's original _plan_ for man.
Patriarch	Abraham	Canaan	Abraham is _chosen_ by God to "father" a _people_ to _represent_ God to the world.
Exodus	Moses	Egypt	Through Moses God _delivers_ the Hebrew people from _slavery_ in Egypt and then gives them the _Law_.
Conquest	Joshua	Canaan	Joshua leads the _conquest_ of the _Promised Land_.
Judges	Samson	Canaan	Samson and others were chosen as _judges_ to _govern_ the people for _400_ rebellious years.
Kingdom	David	Israel	David, the greatest king in the new _monarchy_, is followed by a succession of mostly _unrighteous_ kings, and God eventually _judges_ Israel for her sin, sending her into exile.
Exile	Daniel	Babylonia	Daniel gives _leadership_ and encourages _faithfulness_ among the _exiles_ for the next seventy years.

CHAPTER ELEVEN

THE RETURN ERA

(EZRA—ESTHER)

A NUMBER OF YEARS AGO, NEWSPAPERS AND MAGAZINES WERE awash with the story of Peter Jenkins, who walked across America. He was consumed by the disillusionment of his generation, and he set out to find his country and himself.

His amazing story is one of long hours, days, and weeks of solitude and drudgery punctuated by occasional life-threatening surprises. He faced danger from weather, accidents, wild animals, and people. He almost died in a snow storm, was attacked by animals, and hunted by cruel men who might have killed him if they had caught him.

Many times he wanted to quit his search. Each time, he was befriended by people who restored his body, his soul, and his faith in America. He lost his dog but gained a wife, a new worldview, and a deep appreciation for the grandeur of his country and its people.

Finally, after more than five long and grueling years of walking, he stepped into the Pacific Ocean. His journey was done. When Peter Jenkins walked into the Oregon waters, he was quite a different person from the one who left his home in Alfred, New York. The trials, the time, the solitude, the people, and the physical and mental challenges had transformed him. On his departure, he was little more than a confused boy. On his return, he was a man.

The return of the nation of Israel from seventy years of captivity in Babylonia parallels in many ways the story of Peter Jenkins. The Israelites went into exile a drifting and confused people. They spent agonizing years in solitude, and in physical and mental torment. They were ministered to unexpectedly by people sent from God. They returned to Israel a sobered people. They were home, refocused in their purpose as a nation, ready to begin again the worship of Jehovah: the God of creation, and the God of Israel.

I. **Review:** Fill in the blanks to bring the chart up-to-date with this era.

STORY OF THE OLD TESTAMENT

ERA	FIGURE		STORY LINE SUMMARY
Creation	Adam	Eden	Adam is created by God, but he _sins_ and _destroys_ God's original _plan_ for man.
Patriarch	Abraham	Canaan	*Abraham* is _chosen_ by God to "father" a _people_ to _represent_ God to the world.
Exodus	Moses	Egypt	Through Moses God _delivers_ the Hebrew people from _slavery_ in Egypt and then gives them the _Law_.
Conquest	Joshua	Canaan	*Joshua* leads the _conquest_ of the _Promised Land_.
Judges	Samson	Canaan	*Samson* and others were chosen as _judges_ to _govern_ the people for _400_ rebellious years.
Kingdoms	David	Israel	*David*, the greatest king in the new _monarchy_, is followed by a succession of mostly _unrighteous_ kings, and God eventually _judges_ Israel for her sin, sending her into exile.
Exile	Daniel	Babylon	*Daniel* gives _leadership_ and encourages _faithfulness_ among the _exiles_ for the next seventy years.

ERA	FIGURE		STORY LINE SUMMARY
Return	*Ezra*	*Jerusalem*	To be completed in this chapter.

II. Story Line Summary: *Ezra leads* the people back from *exile* to rebuild *Jerusalem.*

ERA	SUMMARY
Return	Ezra _leads_ the people back from _exile_ to rebuild _Jerusalem._

III. Expansion: There are four major subjects in the Return Era:
1. Disrepair
2. Temple
3. People
4. Walls

1. Disrepair: Destruction from war and neglect
(Nehemiah 1:1–3)

During the seventy years of captivity, the leadership of Judah has been taken into exile, and the city of Jerusalem falls into disrepair. Not only has the city suffered the ravages of the military campaign during the initial conquest, but it has also fallen victim to the erosion of neglect. The *destruction from war and neglect* leaves Jerusalem in a state of abject ruin.

2. Temple: Rebuilding the temple (Ezra 1—6)

God prompts Cyrus, king of Persia, to initiate the financing and rebuilding of the Jewish temple in Jerusalem. Under the direction of Zerubbabel, a notable Jewish figure in Persia, the *rebuilding of the temple* is begun. Considerable opposition from Gentiles around Jerusalem is encountered. At the urging of Haggai and Zechariah, two Jewish prophets living in Jerusalem, the restoration of the temple is completed.

3. People: Spiritual rebuilding (Ezra 7—10)

Rebuilding the temple is a direct parallel to the *spiritual rebuilding* of the Jewish people. Temple worship has been discontinued for seventy years. Most of the Jews have never seen or heard the Law of Moses. They have to be instructed in a national reeducation program. Ezra sets his heart to study the Law of the Lord, to practice it, and to teach God's statutes and ordinances in Israel to rebuild the people as they return from exile.

4. Walls: Restoration complete (Nehemiah)

Even though not all Jews returned when they could have (see the Book of Esther, whose events take place during this Era) many Jews are now back home in Jerusalem. The temple stands restored as the dominant structure in the city, but the walls of the city are still broken down. This is a security threat as well as a source of national humiliation. Nehemiah, another Jewish notable serving Artaxerxes, king of Persia, is burdened to rebuild the walls. He is given permission and financing by the king of Persia to do so. A short time later, the walls frame the noble city of Jerusalem, home of the temple of God. *Restoration is complete* as the temple is rebuilt, the people are rebuilt, and the walls are rebuilt.

SELF-TEST

A. Four Major Subjects in the Return Era

(Write in the correct subject from the options at left.)

OPTIONS:	SUBJECT:	DESCRIPTION:
Disrepair	*People*	Spiritual rebuilding
Temple	*Temple*	Rebuilding the temple
People	*Disrepair*	Destruction from war and neglect
Walls	*Walls*	Restoration complete

B. Story Line Summary

(Fill in the blanks from memory.)

ERA	SUMMARY
Return	Ezra *leads* the people back from *exile* to rebuild *Jerusalem*

87

C. Arc of Bible History

(Fill in the names of the eras.)

1. Creation	5. Judges	9. Silence
2. Patriarch	6. Kingdoms	10. Gospels
3. Exodus	7. Exile	11. Church
4. Conquest	8. Return	12. Missions

D. The Geography of the Return Era

(Draw an arrow from Persia to Jerusalem on the map at the top of the next page to represent geographical movements during the Return Era.)

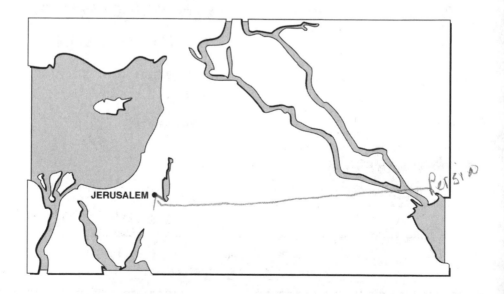

JERUSALEM

Persia

E. Story of the Old Testament

(Fill in the blanks. To check your answers, see the Appendix.)

ERA	FIGURE		STORY LINE SUMMARY
Creation	Adam	Eden	Adam is created by God, but he _sins_ and _destroys_ God's original _plan_ for man.
Patriarch	Abraham	Canaan	*Abraham is* _chosen_ by God to "father" a _people_ to _represent_ God to the world.
Exodus	Moses	Egypt	Through Moses God _delivers_ the Hebrew people from _slavery_ in Egypt and then gives them the _Law_.
Conquest	Joshua	Canaan	*Joshua leads the* _conquest_ of the _Promised Land_.
Judges	Samson	Canaan	*Samson and others were chosen as* _judges_ to _govern_ the people for _400_ rebellious years.
Kingdoms	David	Israel	*David, the greatest king in the* new _monarchy_, is followed by a succession of mostly _unrighteous_ kings, and God eventually _judges_ Israel for her sin, sending her into exile.
Exile	Daniel	Babylon	*Daniel gives* _leadership_ and encourages _faithfulness_ among the _exiles_ for the next seventy years.

ERA	FIGURE		STORY LINE SUMMARY
Return	Ezra	Jerusalem	Ezra _leads_ the people back from _exile_ to rebuild _Jerusalem_.

CHAPTER TWELVE

THE SILENCE ERA

(BETWEEN THE OLD AND NEW TESTAMENTS)

 A LION WHO WAS CAUGHT UP WITH HIS MASTERY OF THE JUNGLE decided to make sure all the other animals knew he was king of the jungle. He was so confident that he bypassed the smaller animals and went straight to the bear. "Who is king of the jungle?" the lion demanded. The bear replied, "Why, you are, of course." The lion gave a mighty roar of approval.

Next, he went to the tiger. "Who is the king of the jungle?" he roared. The tiger quickly responded, "Everyone knows that you are, O mighty lion." The lion swelled with pride.

Next on the list was the elephant. The lion faced the elephant and leveled his question. "Who is king of the jungle?" he challenged. The elephant grabbed the lion with his trunk, whirled him around in the air five or six times, and slammed him against a tree. Then he pounded him on the ground several times, sat on him once, dipped him in the lake, and dumped him out on the shore.

The lion, battered and bruised, struggled to his feet, peered at the elephant through his good eye, and said, "Look, just because you don't know the answer is no reason to get mean about it."

The religious leaders of the Silence Era were very much like the lion. They pretended to have power, and they became self-absorbed. It has been said that some people drink at the fountain of knowledge while others only gargle. All this pride caused a pattern of religious hypocrisy that was leading to self-destruction and made this period one of the more disappointing eras in the nation's history.

I. **Review:** Fill in the blanks to bring the chart up-to-date with this era.

STORY OF THE OLD TESTAMENT

ERA	FIGURE		STORY LINE SUMMARY
Creation	Adam	Eden	Adam is created by God, but he _sins_ and _destroys_ God's original _plan_ for man.
Patriarch	Abraham	Canaan	*Abraham* is _chosen_ by God to "father" a _people_ to _represent_ God to the world.
Exodus	Moses	Egypt	Through Moses God _delivers_ the Hebrew people from _slavery_ in Egypt and then gives them the _Law_.
Conquest	Joshua	Canaan	*Joshua* leads the _conquest_ of the _Promised Land_.
Judges	Samson	Canaan	*Samson* and others were chosen as _judges_ to _govern_ the people for _400_ rebellious years.
Kingdom	David	Israel	*David*, the greatest king in the new _monarch_, is followed by a succession of mostly _unrighteous_ kings, and God eventually _judges_ Israel for her sin, sending her into exile.
Exile	Daniel	Babylonia	*Daniel* gives _leadership_ and encourages _faithfulness_ among the _exiles_ for the next seventy years.

ERA	FIGURE		STORY LINE SUMMARY
Return	*Ezra*	*Jerusalem*	Ezra _lead_ the people back from _exile_ to rebuild _Jerusalem_
Silence	*Pharisees*	*Jerusalem*	To be completed in this chapter.

II. Story Line Summary: *Pharisees* and others *entomb* the *Israelites* in *legalism* for the next *four hundred* years.

ERA	SUMMARY
Silence	*Pharisees* and others _entomb_ the _Israelites_ in _legalism_ for the next _400_ years.

III. Expansion: There are four major subjects in the Silence Era:

1. The Changing Guard
2. Political Sects
3. Religious Sects
4. Messianic Hope

1. The Changing Guard: The march of nations

At the close of the Old Testament, Jerusalem is ruled by Persia. Alexander the Great defeats the Persians in 333 B.C. and establishes Greek culture and the Greek language as a unifying force for that part of the world. When Alexander dies, his kingdom is quartered, but Hellenistic (Greek) culture is still advanced and remains the dominant influence. When Rome conquers that part of the world, Roman influences are introduced but for now the Greek influence is still strong. *The march of nations* passes from Persia to Greece to Rome.

2. Political Sects: The Maccabeans and Zealots

Throughout the four hundred Silent Years, there are militant Jews who attempt to revolt against foreign rule and make Jerusalem and the surrounding area of Judea an independent country. These include the *Maccabeans* and the *Zealots*.

3. Religious Sects: Pharisees and Sadducees

There are two primary religious "parties" in Jerusalem during this time. Unfortunately, neither offers much guidance in true spirituality, as they are caught up in promoting a religious "legalism" of external adherence to rules while overlooking inner motivations and attitudes. The Pharisees are orthodox and conservative, and they foster separation between themselves and "secular" society. The Sadducees are more liberal. They are the party of the Jerusalem aristocracy, and they use their wealth and influence to keep the political waters calm. A ruling board, called the Sanhedrin, is made up of representatives from both the *Pharisees* and *Sadducees*, but the two groups have little in common except their desire for religious freedom and, later, their antagonism for Jesus of Nazareth.

4. Messianic Hope: Expectation of a savior

The "Messiah," or "Savior," is one who is prophesied throughout the Old Testament to come save the Jews. Some feel they need spiritual salvation, and others are looking only for political salvation. For both reasons, the expectation and hope for the coming of the Messiah is strong during the four hundred Silent Years. Events of the Silence Era seem to especially prepare the world for the coming of the Messiah:

(1) This part of the world has a common language and a common culture, which facilitates the spread of a Messianic message.

(2) The Roman Empire has brought this region military peace, an extensive system of roads and sea travel, and a common government so that people can travel extensively without interference.

(3) The Jews are suffering such religious persecution and political humiliation that widespread hope and *expectation of a savior* exists.

These facts make the coming of Jesus of Nazareth, claiming to be the Messiah, an event that captures the attention of the entire Jewish world.

SELF-TEST

A. Four Major Subjects in the Silence Era

(Write in the correct subject from the options at left.)

OPTIONS:	SUBJECT:	DESCRIPTION:
The Changing Guard	*Religious Sects*	Pharisees and Sadducees
Political Sects	*The Changing Guard*	The march of nations
Religious Sects	*Messianic Hope*	Expectations of a savior
Messianic Hope	*Political Sects*	Maccabeans and Zealots

B. Story Line Summary

(Fill in the blanks from memory.)

ERA	SUMMARY
Silence	*Pharisees* and others _entomb_ the _Israelites_ in _legalism_ for the next _400_ years.

C. Arc of Bible History

(Fill in the names of the eras. To check your answers, see the Appendix.)

1. Creation	5. Judges	9. Silence
2. Patriarch	6. Kingdoms	10. Gospels
3. Exodus	7. Exile	11. Church
4. Conquest	8. Return	12. Missions

95

D. The Geography of the Silence Era

(Put a 1 next to Persia, a 2 next to Greece, and a 3 next to Rome. Then draw an arrow from Persia to Greece to Rome, to represent the geographical movement of the Silence Era.)

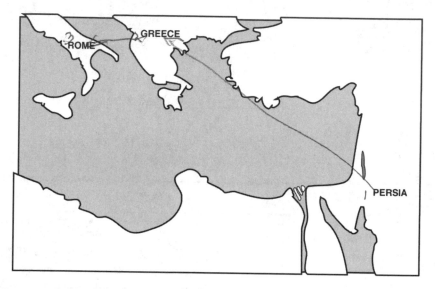

E. Story of the Old Testament

(Fill in the blanks.)

ERA	FIGURE		STORY LINE SUMMARY
Creation	Adam	Eden	Adam is created by God, but he __sins__ and __destroys__ God's original __plan__ for man.
Patriarch	Abraham	Canaan	Abraham is __chosen__ by God to "father" a __people__ to __represent__ God to the world.
Exodus	Moses	Egypt	Through Moses God __delivers__ the Hebrew people from __slavery__ in Egypt and then gives them the __Law__.

ERA	FIGURE		STORY LINE SUMMARY
Conquest	Joshua	Canaan	Joshua leads the _Conquest_ of the _Promised land_.
Judges	Samson	Canaan	Samson and others were chosen as _judges_ to _govern_ the people for _480 years_ rebellious years.
Kingdoms	David	Israel	David, the greatest king in the new _monarch_, is followed by a succession of mostly _unrighteous_ kings, and God eventually _judges_ Israel for her sin, sending her into exile.
Exile	Daniel	Babylonia	Daniel gives _leadership_ and encourages _faithfulness_ among the _exiles_ for the next seventy years.
Return	Ezra	Jerusalem	Ezra _leads_ the people back from _exile_ to rebuild _Jerusalem_.
Silence	Pharisees	Jerusalem	Pharisees and others _entomb_ the _Israelite_ in _legalism_ for the next _400 yrs_ years.

Congratulations! You have just passed another milestone! You have completed the overview of the Historical Books of the Old Testament, the ones that tell the story of the Old Testament. Now we will take a look at the Poetical Books and the Prophetical Books in the next two chapters.

CHAPTER THIRTEEN

THE POETICAL BOOKS

(JOB—SONG OF SOLOMON)

IT IS NO SECRET THAT, HISTORICALLY SPEAKING, POETS HAVE "marched to the beat of a different drummer," and not everyone has appreciated their poetry. Charles Babbage, a British mathematician, objected to Alfred Lord Tennyson's line from "The Vision of Sin": "Every moment dies a man, / Every moment one is born," saying that if that were true, "the population of the world would be at a standstill." In the interest of accuracy, he wrote to Tennyson, the lines should be amended to read, "Every moment dies a man, / Every moment one and one-sixteenth is born."

Those who like poetry either think they can write it or wish they could. It is much more difficult to write enduring poetry than one imagines, however, and amateur attempts are rarely widely appreciated. Euripides once confessed that it had taken him three days to write three verses. His astonished friend, a poet of lesser abilities, exclaimed, "I could have written a hundred in that time!" "I believe it," replied Euripides, "but they would have lived only three days."

King Louis XIV showed Nicolas Beaulieu, a French poet of the day, some poems he had written and asked his opinion of them. The great poet was also an accomplished diplomat: "Sire, nothing is impossible for Your Majesty. Your Majesty has set out to write bad verses and has succeeded."

Poetry is a song of the soul. Wherever great civilizations have existed, poetry has been written, and the poetry of Israel is among the finest. The psalms of David and the proverbs of Solomon stand up well when compared with any body of poetry ever written.

I. Review: We remind ourselves that there are three kinds of books in the Old Testament: Historical, Poetical, and Prophetical. There are five Poetical Books that follow the first seventeen Historical Books, as seen below.

THE THREE KINDS OF BOOKS IN THE OLD TESTAMENT

Historical	*Poetical*	*Prophetical*
Genesis	Job	Isaiah
Exodus	Psalms	Jeremiah
Leviticus	Proverbs	Lamentations
Numbers	Ecclesiastes	Ezekiel
Deuteronomy	Song of Solomon	Daniel
Joshua		Hosea
Judges		Joel
Ruth		Amos
1 Samuel		Obadiah
2 Samuel		Jonah
1 Kings		Micah
2 Kings		Nahum
1 Chronicles		Habakkuk
2 Chronicles		Zephaniah
Ezra		Haggai
Nehemiah		Zechariah
Esther		Malachi

To review, history has now come to an end. The Historical Books are completed, and the books of poetry of the people of Israel begin. The Poetical Books, the middle five books of the Old Testament, can be located in the time line constructed by the Historical Books. Job was written during the time of the events of the Book of Genesis; Psalms, during the life of David in 2 Samuel; and Proverbs, Ecclesiastes, and Song of Solomon were written during the lifetime of Solomon in the time covered in 1 Kings. See the following figure for a visual representation.

Poetical Books

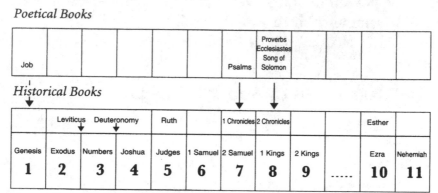

Historical Books

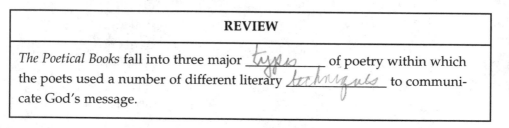

II. Overview Summary: *The Poetical Books* fall into three major *types* of poetry within which the poets used a number of different literary *techniques* to communicate God's message.

REVIEW

The Poetical Books fall into three major __*types*__ of poetry within which the poets used a number of different literary __*techniques*__ to communicate God's message.

The three major types of Hebrew poetry are:

1. *Lyric poetry*—to be *accompanied by music*, like a song.

2. *Instructional poetry*—to *teach principles of living* through pithy maxims.

3. *Dramatic poetry*—a narrative that *tells a story* in poetic form.

REVIEW OF THE THREE MAJOR TYPES OF HEBREW POETRY

1.   *Lyric poetry*—to be *accompanied by music*, like a song. *Psalms*

2.   *Instructional poetry*—to *teach principles of living* through pithy maxims. *Proverbs*

3.   *Dramatic poetry*—a narrative that *tells a story* in poetic form. *Job*

The two main literary techniques are

1. *Parallelism*
2. *Figures of speech*

1. Parallelism: The matching of ideas

Summary Definition: Rather than matching sounds, a Hebrew poet was more concerned with *matching ideas*, a technique called "parallelism."

REVIEW
Rather than matching sounds, a Hebrew poet was more concerned with *matching ideas*, a technique called "parallelism."

Six of the most common forms of parallelism are:

1. *Synonymous parallelism:* The ideas presented are similar.
   > Make me know Thy ways, O LORD;
   > Teach me Thy paths. (Psalm 25:4)

2. *Synthetic parallelism:* The second thought completes the first thought.
   > The Lord is my shepherd,
   > I shall not want. (Psalm 23:1)

3. *Antithetic parallelism:* The second thought contrasts with the first.
   > For the Lord knows the way of the righteous,
   > But the way of the wicked shall perish. (Psalm 1:6)

4. *Emblematic parallelism:* The first line uses a figure of speech to illustrate the idea stated in the second line.
   > As the deer pants for the water brooks,
   > So my soul pants for Thee, O God. (Psalm 42:1)

5. *Climactic parallelism:* The second line repeats the first with the exception of the last word or words.
   > It is not for kings, O Lemuel,
   > It is not for kings to drink wine. (Proverbs 31:4)

6. *Formal parallelism:* Both lines of poetry must exist for a complete thought.

> But as for Me, I have installed My King
> Upon Zion, My holy mountain. (Psalm 2:6)

REVIEW

(Fill in the blanks from the options listed.)

1. In synonymous parallelism, the ideas are __b__.
    a. ridiculous.
    b. similar.
    c. spelled the same.

2. In synthetic parallelism, __b__.
    a. the second thought is made of nylon.
    b. the second thought completes the first.
    c. the second thought doesn't exist.

3. In antithetic parallelism, __b__.
    a. the second thought is written backward.
    b. the second thought contrasts with the first.
    c. the first thought has no counterpart in the universe.

4. In emblematic parallelism, __b__.
    a. a small metallic emblem is affixed to the first line.
    b. a figure of speech in the first line illustrates the idea in the second line.
    c. the ideas are drawn in primitive art form.

5. In climactic parallelism, __b__.
    a. the second thought is very cold.
    b. the second line repeats the first with the exception of the last word or words.
    c. the thought is completed in the third act.

6. In formal parallelism, __b__.
    a. the first line appears in a black tie.
    b. both lines of poetry must exist for a complete thought.
    c. the second line doesn't slurp its soup.

(The answer to all the above questions is the first letter in the word basketball.)

2. Figures of Speech: Creating visual images

Summary Definition: Since the Hebrew poets wanted mental pictures to pop into the reader's mind, a prime consideration was *creating visual images,* which they accomplished with vivid "figures of speech."

REVIEW

Since the Hebrew poets wanted mental pictures to pop into the reader's mind, a prime consideration was _Creating visual images_, which they accomplished with vivid "figures of speech."

Five of the most common figures of speech are:

1. *Simile:* a comparison between two unlike things.
   Keep me as the apple of the eye. (Psalm 17:8)

2. *Metaphor:* a comparison in which one thing is said to be another. *has helping verb*
   The LORD is my shepherd. (Psalm 23:1)

3. *Hyperbole:* deliberate overstatement for the sake of emphasis.
   Every night I make my bed swim,
   I dissolve my couch with my tears. (Psalm 6:6)

4. *Rhetorical question:* asking a question for the purpose of making a statement.
   Who can speak of the mighty deeds of the LORD,
   Or can show forth all His praise? (Psalm 106:2)

5. *Personification:* assigning the characteristics of a human to lifeless objects.
   The sun knows the place of its setting. (Psalm 104:19)

While there are other figures of speech, these are the most notable. The ones listed here, in particular, express the visual imagery to which the Hebrew poets were committed in order to cause mental pictures to pop into our minds.

If you can get away from the need to hear rhyme and rhythm, you can gain an appreciation for Hebrew poetry. These men were "wordsmiths" and "thoughtsmiths" who played with words and ideas, contrasting them, comparing them, completing them in ways that lifted them above mere prose.

III. **Expansion:** The Five Poetical Books
1. Job
2. Psalms
3. Proverbs
4. Ecclesiastes
5. Song of Solomon

1. Job: Suffering and God's sovereignty

Job is a very wealthy, godly man whose fortunes are suddenly and dramatically reversed. He loses his health, his wealth, and his family and is plunged into profound suffering. The book presents, in "dramatic poetry," the internal struggles of Job, and a series of debates with three friends trying to gain a proper perspective on *suffering and God's sovereignty*. In the end, God reveals His majesty and power. Though Job's questions are never answered, he willingly submits to the sovereignty of God, and his fortunes are restored and doubled.

2. Psalms: Praise in public worship

Psalm means "book of praises." The Book of Psalms is a collection of 150 psalms that are divided into five smaller "books." The Psalms are used as a book of prayer and *praise in public worship* in the tabernacle, temple, and synagogues. There are three primary types of psalms: praise, thanksgiving, and lament. King David writes almost half of them, while several different authors complete the rest.

3. Proverbs: Wisdom, skill for living

The purpose of proverbs is to impart *wisdom*, or *"skill for living."* More specifically, they highlight practical wisdom, discernment, self-discipline, and moral courage. This "instructional poetry" is written in short, pithy maxims focusing on one's relationship to God and others—money, morals, speech, industry, honesty, etc. The message is that a life of wisdom and righteousness should preempt a life of foolishness and unrighteousness.

4. Ecclesiastes: Futility of temporal pursuits

Solomon, with his unlimited resources and opportunity, tries to find meaning in life through industry, pleasure, wealth, wisdom, and power, and finds them all unsatisfying. After he reviews these efforts and the *futility of temporal pursuits*, he concludes in this "instructional poetry" that there is only one thing that can satisfy man: to "fear God and keep His commandments" (12:13).

5. Song of Solomon: God's marriage manual

The Song of Solomon is *God's marriage manual*. This "dramatic poetry" pictures the intimate love relationship between Solomon and his Shulammite bride. In doing so, it presents God's perspective on married love.

SELF-TEST

The Five Poetical Books
(Write in the correct book from the options at left.)

OPTIONS:	BOOK:	DESCRIPTION:
Job	*Ecclesiastes*	Futility of temporal pursuits
Psalms	*Job*	Suffering and God's sovereignty
Proverbs	*Solomon*	God's marriage manual
Ecclesiastes	*Psalms*	Praise in public worship
Song of Solomon	*Proverbs*	Wisdom; skill for living

CHAPTER FOURTEEN

THE PROPHETICAL BOOKS

(ISAIAH—MALACHI)

PROPHECY GETS A GRIP ON US LIKE NOTHING ELSE. WE ARE mesmerized and spellbound by it. What does the future hold? That question grabs us by the collar, throws us up against the wall, sinks its thumbs into our jugular, and holds us there for an answer. Some look into crystal balls, read tea leaves, study astrological charts, and consult prophets for a glimpse into the unknown. From "When will the world end?" to "What should I wear tomorrow?" they hunger to probe into the depths of that which has not yet happened.

There is an intuitive sense that a veil hangs between the human and the divine, and that prophets will help us peer beyond the veil. Outside of the Bible, however, prophets have had an uneven track record. Croesus lived in the sixth century B.C. and was king of Lydia in Asia Minor. Deliberating whether to attack the Persian Empire, he asked the oracle at Delphi if the undertaking would prosper. The oracle replied that if he went to war, he would destroy a great empire. Encouraged, Croesus invaded the Persian realms. He was decisively beaten, and the Persians then invaded Lydia, captured its capital, and threw Croesus himself into chains. Croesus again sent an emissary to Delphi, this time with the question, "Why did you deceive me?" The priestess of the oracle replied that she had not deceived him—Croesus had indeed destroyed a great empire.

Girolamo Cardano, an Italian mathematician of the sixteenth century, was known throughout Europe as an astrologer, even visiting England to cast the horoscope of the young king, Edward VI. A steadfast believer in the accuracy of his so-called science, Cardano constructed a horoscope predicting the hour of his own death.

When the day dawned, it found him in good health and safe from harm. Rather than have his prediction fail, Cardano killed himself.

Biblical prophets find themselves in a different league, however, from the run-of-the-mill prophets. If a man was a true prophet from God, no prediction of his would ever fail. If a prophet ever voiced a prophecy that failed, he was to be stoned to death. This discouraged the impostors and made the biblical prophets highly reliable. There were many true prophets in the Old Testament, but not all of them committed their messages to writings that were preserved. In the Bible, we have sixteen men who wrote down their messages. These writings are called the Prophetical Books, and they comprise the final seventeen books of the Old Testament, as seen in the review below.

I. Review:

STRUCTURE OF THE OLD TESTAMENT

Historical	Poetical	Prophetical
17	*5*	*17*
Genesis	Job	Isaiah
Exodus	Psalms	Jeremiah
Leviticus	Proverbs	Lamentations
Numbers	Ecclesiastes	Ezekiel
Deuteronomy	Song of Solomon	Daniel
Joshua		Hosea
Judges		Joel
Ruth		Amos
1 Samuel		Obadiah
2 Samuel		Jonah
1 Kings		Micah
2 Kings		Nahum
1 Chronicles		Habakkuk
2 Chronicles		Zephaniah
Ezra		Haggai
Nehemiah		Zechariah
Esther		Malachi

Our history is completed. From Genesis, the first Historical Book, to Nehemiah, the last Historical Book, we stretched out a time line that told the story of ancient Israel. Then we dropped the Poetical Books in their proper place. Now we do the same with the Prophetical Books, as seen below.

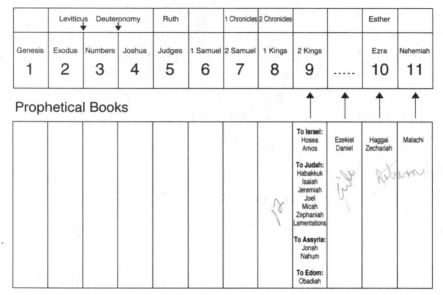

Historical Books

	Leviticus	Deuteronomy		Ruth		1 Chronicles	2 Chronicles			Esther	
Genesis	Exodus	Numbers	Joshua	Judges	1 Samuel	2 Samuel	1 Kings	2 Kings		Ezra	Nehemiah
1	2	3	4	5	6	7	8	9	-----	10	11

Prophetical Books

To Israel:
Hosea
Amos

To Judah:
Habakkuk
Isaiah
Jeremiah
Joel
Micah
Zephaniah
Lamentations

To Assyria:
Jonah
Nahum

To Edom:
Obadiah

Ezekiel
Daniel

Haggai
Zechariah

Malachi

Twelve of the Prophetical Books were written during the time covered in the Book of 2 Kings, which records the decline of the nations of Israel and Judah. This is because the primary message of the prophets was to the nations to stop sinning and return to the Lord. The prophets predicted what would happen to the nations if the people did not heed the warning. Of the remaining books, two prophets (Ezekiel and Daniel) ministered during the Exile, and three (Haggai, Zechariah, and Malachi) during the return.

II. Overview Summary: *Prophecy* is *proclaiming* the Word of God, both for the *future* and in the *present*.

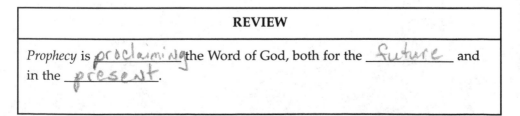

REVIEW
Prophecy is proclaiming the Word of God, both for the future and in the present.

III. Expansion: There are four main features of the Prophetical writings:

1. Designation
2. Time Period
3. Foretelling
4. Forthtelling

1. Designation: Major and minor prophets

In recent history, the Prophetical Books have had two designations: *major prophets* and *minor prophets*. The major prophets are the first five Prophetical Books: Isaiah, Jeremiah, Lamentations, Ezekiel, and Daniel. The minor prophets are the remaining twelve. The major prophets are called "major" because they are longer books, while the others are called "minor" because they are shorter writings than the major prophets.

2. Time Period: Pre-Exile, Exile, or Post-Exile

The Prophetical Books are divided into three chronological periods: *Pre-Exile*, *Exile*, and *Post-Exile*. Most of the prophetical ministries and books occur before the Exile. Three prophets, Haggai, Zechariah, and Malachi, prophesy during the return. Of those who prophesy before the Exile, two prophesy primarily to Israel (the northern kingdom), seven primarily to Judah (the southern kingdom), and three to other countries, as seen in the following lists.

STRUCTURE OF THE PROPHETICAL BOOKS

Pre-Exile

TO ISRAEL:	TO JUDAH:	TO ASSYRIA:	TO EDOM:
Hosea	Habakkuk	Jonah	Obadiah
Amos	Isaiah	Nahum	
	Jeremiah		
	Joel		
	Micah		
	Zephaniah		
	Lamentations		

Exile	*Post-Exile*
FROM BABYLONIA:	TO JERUSALEM:
Ezekiel	Haggai
Daniel	Zechariah
	Malachi

3. Foretelling: Predicting the future

The most famous characteristic of a prophet is that he can occasionally *predict the future*. This is not an ability inherent within himself. Rather, this information is given to him by God. In Israel, the test of a true prophet is that he must be 100 percent accurate. If a prophet ever says anything that does not come true, he is not a prophet of God. And the penalty for giving a prophecy that does not come true is death by stoning. This keeps the ranks of the prophets pure.

4. Forthtelling: Proclaiming the teachings of God

While the ministry of "foretelling" (telling the future) is more dramatic, the ministry of "forthtelling" is vastly more common in the life of a prophet. Forthtelling means simply *proclaiming the teachings of God* to the people. Primarily it relates to righteous living. There are three characteristics of this part of a prophet's ministry.

1. Exposing sin and calling people to a higher moral lifestyle.
2. Warning of judgment if the people don't reform.
3. Proclaiming the coming Messiah.

The prophets usually warned about judgments related to the nation of Israel or Judah being militarily conquered and taken out of the land.

SELF-TEST

A. Four Main Features of the Prophetical Books
(Write in the correct feature from the options at left.)

OPTIONS:	FEATURE:	DESCRIPTION:
Designation	*Foretelling*	Predicting the future
Time Period	*Forthtelling*	Proclaiming the teachings of God
Foretelling	*Time Period*	Pre-Exile, Exile, Post-Exile
Forthtelling	*Designation*	Major and minor prophets

B. The Geography of the Prophetical Books

The primary locations in which prophets ministered are found on the map below. Match the country with the location by filling in the blanks according to the numbers.

1. Israel
2. Judah
3. Edom

4. Assyria
5. Babylonia
6. Jerusalem

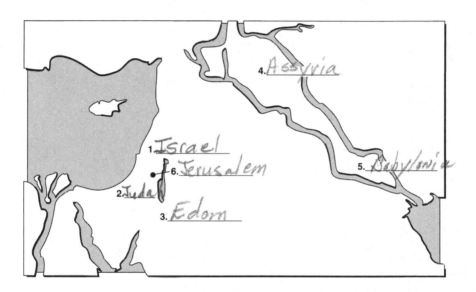

Wonderful! You have now completed Section 1, the Story of the Old Testament. This is a major milestone in understanding the Bible. The remaining sections have been structured so that they are challenging, but not overwhelming. If you completed the Old Testament, you can complete the entire book, and you're almost halfway through!

Now, having just overviewed the Poetical and Prophetical Books of the Old Testament and having seen where they fit into the Story of the Bible, we are ready to continue that story as we begin Section 2, the Story of the New Testament.

SECTION TWO

THE STORY OF THE NEW TESTAMENT

CHAPTER FIFTEEN

THE GEOGRAPHY AND STRUCTURE OF THE NEW TESTAMENT

 HIDING AMONG THE GIANT ANDES MOUNTAINS IN THE SOUTH American country of Peru lies a flat valley about forty miles long, isolated from the rest of the world. Roads and paths lie all over the floor of this vast valley, strewn like long, thin trees that have fallen at random. For years, archaeologists have guessed that they were a forgotten network of roads, left by an ancient civilization.

Perspective was changed radically, however, when someone chanced to study the valley from the air. From this vantage point, what seemed to be haphazard and random now became quite clear. They were not roads and paths at all, but a monumental desert mural picturing objects that were many miles in height. What the murals are, what they mean, how they were built, for whom they were built, and by whom they were built are all lost to the mist of time.

The monumental mural has a symbolic message for us all, however. Often, the whole picture of something cannot be seen if we are too close to it. We must get back away from the details of what we are studying to see the overview.

This is certainly true of the geography of the New Testament. When in the Gospels you read of going from the cities of Jericho to Jerusalem to Cana, those are just words on a page with no meaning until you have overviewed the geography. You have no realization that someone has just walked seventy-five miles (the distance from Baltimore to Philadelphia) or that the trip also included walking up thirteen hundred feet in altitude and then down another one thousand.

In fact, gaining perspective on the geography of the New Testament is in itself a fascinating study. Israel is a tiny country compared to the United States. Draw a line fifty miles wide from New York to Boston, or stand Massachusetts on end, or shrink New Hampshire by 10 percent, and you have the approximate land area of Israel.

Yet it is a remarkably varied land. From low desert to high mountain, with lush valleys and rolling hills in between, the gamut is run in topography. Any body of water that you cannot swim across is a "sea," and every hill higher than your head is a "mountain." The Sea of Galilee is seven miles by fourteen miles, almost a mud puddle compared to the Great Lakes. The Dead Sea is ten miles by fifty miles, smaller than some virtually nameless reservoirs in the U.S. The "mighty" Jordan is little more than a strong-running creek compared to the truly mighty rivers of the world like the Amazon or Mississippi. Perhaps because it is such a small country, everything is exaggerated.

To be able to create mental pictures as you read the events in the New Testament is to help the narrative come alive. So, as we begin looking at the New Testament, we begin with the geography.

THE GEOGRAPHY OF THE GOSPELS

The difference between the geography of the Gospels and the geography of the Book of Acts is significant enough to warrant separate treatment.

Bodies of Water

Once you have mastered the geography of the Old Testament, the geography of the New Testament is fairly simple. The bodies of water are among those of the Old Testament studied in Chapter 2. (To review, go to the map that follows and write in the name of the bodies of water by matching the numbers.)

1. Mediterranean Sea
2. Sea of Galilee
3. Jordan River
4. Dead Sea

BODIES OF WATER IN THE GOSPELS

(Fill in the appropriate blanks on the following map. The names and numbers should match those on the preceding list.)

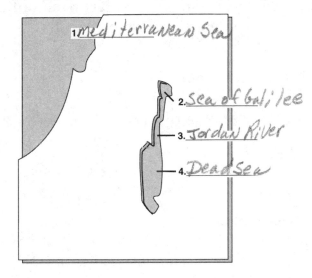

1. Mediterranean Sea
2. Sea of Galilee
3. Jordan River
4. Dead Sea

Provinces and Cities

The primary geographical area in the Gospels is the same as that which was ruled by the nation of Israel in the Old Testament. However, the land, now known as Palestine, is ruled by Rome and has been divided into sections, or provinces. (*As you read these descriptions, write the location on the map that follows by matching the letters.*)

A. The Province of Galilee

Located between the Mediterranean Sea and the sea that shares its name, Galilee, is the province Jesus considered His home province. Both Nazareth, His early home, and Capernaum, His later home, are in Galilee. Hence the phrase "the man from Galilee."

B. The Province of Samaria

Located between the Mediterranean Sea and the Jordan River, Samaria is home to Samaritans. Part Jewish, part Gentile people, they live in constant animosity with the Jews.

C. The Province of Judea

Located between the Mediterranean Sea and the Dead Sea, Judea is approximately the same area as the southern tribe of Judah in the Old Testament. Encompassing the city of Jerusalem, it is home to most of the Jews in the New Testament.

D. The Province of Perea

A long, narrow province on the east bank of the Jordan River, Jesus spent some concentrated time there with His disciples toward the end of His ministry.

E. The City of Nazareth

Located in Galilee just west of the Sea of Galilee, it is the town where Mary and Joseph lived, and in which Jesus grew up.

F. The City of Capernaum

Located on the very top of the Sea of Galilee, it is where Jesus called home during His ministry years.

G. The City of Jerusalem

Located in Judea, just off the top of the Dead Sea, it is the home of the temple, the holy city, and the center of activity for Jews.

H. The City of Bethlehem

The birthplace of Jesus, it is five miles southwest of Jerusalem.

PROVINCES AND CITIES OF THE GOSPELS

(Fill in the appropriate blanks below. The letters and names should match those from the list above.)

THE GEOGRAPHY OF ACTS

Bodies of water

The bodies of water are the same as for the Gospels, only more of the Mediterranean is involved. Therefore, you already know them.

Countries and Cities

As we move out of the Gospels and into Acts, our geography expands from Palestine further into the Roman Empire. (*As you read the descriptions, write the location on the map that follows.*)

1. The Country of Galatia

Located in modern-day Turkey, it was the destination of the apostle Paul's first missionary journey to take the gospel message to Gentiles.

2. The Country of Greece

Located in modern Greece, it was the destination for Paul's second missionary journey.

3. The Country of Asia

Located on the western coast of modern Turkey, it was the destination of Paul's third missionary journey.

4. The Country of Italy

Located in modern Italy, it was the country of Paul's final imprisonment and death.

5. The City of Jerusalem

Located in modern Jerusalem, it is the location of the beginning of the early Christian Church.

6. The City of Damascus

Located in modern Damascus, in the modern country of Syria, it was Paul's destination when he was temporarily blinded by Jesus and converted to Christianity.

7. The City of Caesarea

Located on the Mediterranean coast just south of the Sea of Galilee, it was the site of Paul's trials.

8. The City of Antioch

On the Mediterranean coast north of Israel, near modern Turkey, it was the beginning point for all three of Paul's missionary journeys.

9. The City of Rome

Located in modern Rome, it was the political and cultural heart of the Roman Empire.

THE GEOGRAPHY OF ACTS

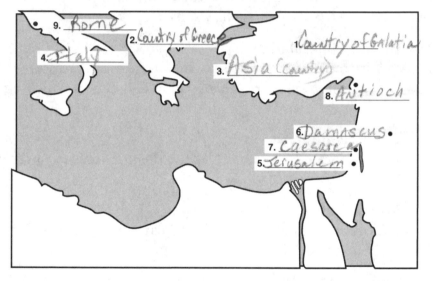

SELF-TEST

The Geography of the Gospels

(Now, from the options listed, fill in the bodies of water, provinces, and cities on the map that follows.)

Numbers = bodies of water	*Letters = cities and provinces*
Dead Sea	Bethlehem
Jordan River	Capernaum
Mediterranean Sea	Galilee
Sea of Galilee	Jerusalem
	Judea
	Nazareth
	Perea
	Samaria

1. *Mediterranean Sea*

F. *Capernaum*

A. *Galilee*

2. *Sea of Galilee*

E.

B. *Samaria*

3. *Jordan River*

G. *Jerusalem*

D. *Perea*

H. *Bethlehem*

4. *Dead Sea*

C. *Judea*

THE GEOGRAPHY OF ACTS

(From the options listed, fill in the countries and cities on the following map.)

Countries:
Asia
Galatia
Greece
Italy

Cities:
Antioch
Caesarea
Damascus
Jerusalem
Rome

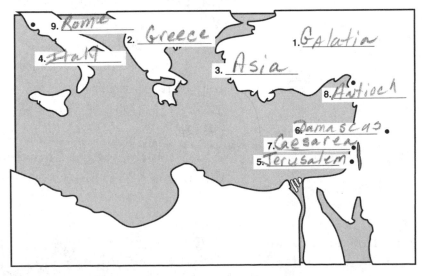

9. *Rome*

2. *Greece*

1. *Galatia*

4. *Italy*

3. *Asia*

8. *Antioch*

6. *Damascus*

7. *Caesarea*

5. *Jerusalem*

THE HISTORICAL BOOKS OF THE NEW TESTAMENT

Having mastered the geography of the New Testament, we are now ready to continue the story of the Bible with the three main eras that remain. You will recall that the twenty-seven books of the New Testament can be divided into three different kinds of books: five Historical Books, thirteen Pauline Epistles, and nine General Epistles.

As we did with the Historical Books in the Old Testament, first we will overview the events of the Historical Books of the New Testament, the Gospels and Acts. Then, in the following chapters, we will expand the story line.

THE THREE MAIN ERAS OF THE NEW TESTAMENT

1. Gospels
The life of Jesus of Nazareth as told in the *Gospels*.

2. Church
The formation of the Christian *Church*.

3. Missions
The expansion of the Church into the Roman Empire through *missions*.

REVIEW

Write in the correct era on the proper line matching the description.

OPTIONS:	ERA:	DESCRIPTION:
Missions	*Gospel*	The life of Jesus of Nazareth, as told in the *Gospels*
Gospel	*Church*	The formation of the Christian *Church*
Church	*Missions*	The expansion of the Church into the Roman Empire through *missions*

We are now able to add this new information to our story line chart from the Old Testament, as seen on the following page.

STORY OF THE BIBLE

ERA	FIGURE		STORY LINE SUMMARY
Creation	Adam	Eden	Adam is created by God, but he sins and destroys God's original plan for man.
Patriarch	Abraham	Canaan	Abraham is chosen by God to "father" a people to represent God to the world.
Exodus	Moses	Egypt	Through Moses God delivers the Hebrew people from slavery in Egypt and then gives them the Law.
Conquest	Joshua	Canaan	Joshua leads the conquest of the Promised Land.
Judges	Samson	Canaan	Samson and others were chosen as judges to govern the people for four hundred rebellious years.
Kingdom	David	Israel	David, the greatest king in the new monarchy, is followed by a succession of mostly unrighteous kings, and God eventually judges Israel for her sin, sending her into exile.
Exile	Daniel	Babylonia	Daniel gives leadership and encourages faithfulness among the exiles for the next seventy years.
Return	Ezra	Jerusalem	Ezra leads the people back from exile to rebuild Jerusalem.
Silence	Pharisees	Jerusalem	Pharisees and others entomb the Israelites in legalism for the next four hundred years.

ERA	FIGURE	LOCATION	
Gospels	To be supplied later.	To be supplied later.	To be supplied later.
Church	To be supplied later.	To be supplied later.	To be supplied later.
Missions	To be supplied later.	To be supplied later.	To be supplied later.

THE THREE CENTRAL FIGURES OF THE NEW TESTAMENT

ERA:	FIGURE:	DESCRIPTION:
Gospels	Jesus	The predicted *Messiah*
Church	Peter	The *leader* of the early Church
Missions	Paul	The first Christian *missionary*

REVIEW

Fill in the blanks.

ERA:	FIGURE:	DESCRIPTION:
Gospels	Jesus	The predicted *Messiah*
Church	Peter	The *leader* of the early Church
Missions	Paul	The first Christian *missionary*

We are now able to add the central figures from the New Testament to our story line chart, which shows just the New Testament Eras.

ERA	FIGURE	LOCATION	STORY LINE SUMMARY
Gospels	*Jesus*	To be supplied later.	To be supplied later.
Church	*Peter*	To be supplied later.	To be supplied later.
Missions	*Paul*	To be supplied later.	To be supplied later.

Our final task is to identify the general or primary geographic location of the events of the three main eras of the New Testament. As an exercise in memory, write in each main era and central historical figure as you read the description of the geographical location.

THE THREE MAIN LOCATIONS OF THE NEW TESTAMENT

ERA:	FIGURE:	LOCATION:	DESCRIPTION:
Gospels *Jesus*		Palestine	The general land area that was known as Canaan and Israel in the Old Testament is commonly known as Palestine in the New. It includes the Roman provinces of Galilee, Samaria, and Judea.
Church *Peter*		Jerusalem	The ancient city of Jerusalem has been in the same location throughout most of biblical history after the Kingdom Era. It is the city that gave birth to the early Church.
Missions *Paul*		Roman Empire	As Paul spread the message of Christianity he took it to the heart of the Roman Empire. From Palestine, north into what is modern Turkey, and west through modern Greece, to Italy.

REVIEW

(Now, from the options listed at right, write in the location to match the era and figure.)

ERA:	FIGURE:	LOCATION:	OPTIONS:
Gospels	Jesus	*Palestine*	Roman Empire
Church	Peter	*Jerusalem*	Palestine
Missions	Paul	*Roman Empire*	Jerusalem

We are now able to add the main locations from the New Testament to our story line chart, as seen in the following.

ERA	FIGURE	LOCATION	STORY LINE SUMMARY
Gospels	*Jesus*	Palestine	To be supplied later.
Church	*Peter*	Jerusalem	To be supplied later.
Missions	*Paul*	Roman Empire	To be supplied later.

ARC OF BIBLE HISTORY

(Fill in the names of the eras. To check your answers, see the Appendix.)

1. Creation	5. Judges	9. Silence
2. Patriarch	6. Kingdom	10. Gospels
3. Exodus	7. Exile	11. Church
4. Conquest	8. Return	12. Missions

From memory fill in the New Testament story line chart.

ERA	FIGURE	LOCATION	STORY LINE SUMMARY
Gospels	Jesus	Palestine	To be supplied later.
Church	Peter	Jerusalem	To be supplied later.
Missions	Paul	Roman Empire	To be supplied later.

Congratulations! You have just taken a big step toward mastering an overview of the New Testament. From now on, we will get more specific, but you have the basic structure well in hand.

CHAPTER SIXTEEN

THE GOSPEL ERA

(MATTHEW—JOHN)

 DR. RICHARD SELZER IS A BRILLIANT SURGEON WHO WROTE A penetrating book entitled *Mortal Lessons: Notes on the Art of Surgery*. In it he writes:

I stand by the bed where a young woman lies, her face postoperative, her mouth twisted in a palsy, clownish. A tiny twig of a facial nerve, the one to the muscles of her mouth, has been severed. She will be thus from now on. The surgeon had followed with religious fervor the curve of her flesh; I promise you that. Nevertheless to remove the tumor in her cheek, I had to cut the little nerve.

Her husband is in the room. He stands on the opposite side of the bed, and together, they seem to dwell in the evening lamplight. Isolated from me, private. Who are they, I ask myself, he and this wry-mouth I have made, who gaze at each other, and touch each other generously, greedily?

The young woman speaks. "Will I always be like this?" she asks. "Yes," I say. "It is because the nerve was cut." She nods and is silent. But the young man smiles. "I like it," he says. "It's kind of cute."

All at once I know who he is. I understand, and I lower my gaze. One is not bold in an encounter with a god. Unmindful, he bends to kiss her crooked mouth, and I am so close I can see how he twists his own lips to accommodate hers, to show that their kiss still works. I remember that the gods appeared in ancient Greece as mortals, and I hold my breath and let the wonder in.

That is the spirit of Jesus. Man's link with God had been severed through sin. And He twisted Himself to accommodate us, and gave us the kiss of eternal life. But to do so He gave His own life on our behalf. Jesus. At the same time, so tender and powerful. The most remarkable figure ever to have lived. And why not? He was God incarnate.

The birth of Jesus split history like a thunderbolt on a hot July evening. Everything before His birth we call B.C., before Christ. Everything after, we call A.D., anno Domini, in the year of our Lord. His story, predicted throughout the Old Testament, is told in the four Gospels: Matthew, Mark, Luke, and John. While the Gospels are biographical, they are actually thematic portraits of Christ's life that place very little emphasis on His early life and great emphasis on the last week of His life. The Gospels tend to follow the chronology of His life, but not slavishly. Not all the Gospels cover the same events in His life. When all four Gospels are put together and "harmonized," only about fifty days of Jesus' active ministry are dealt with.

I. Review: Fill in the blanks to begin the chart for this era.

STORY OF THE NEW TESTAMENT

ERA	FIGURE		STORY LINE SUMMARY
Gospels	Jesus	Palestine	To be supplied later.

II. Story Line Summary: *Jesus* comes in fulfillment of the Old Testament *prophecies* of a savior and offers *salvation* and the true kingdom of God. While some accept Him, most *reject* Him, and He is crucified, buried, and resurrected.

ERA	SUMMARY
Gospel	*Jesus* comes in fulfillment of the Old Testament prophecies of a savior and offers salvation and the true kingdom of God. While some accept Him, most reject Him, and He is crucified, buried, and resurrected.

III. Expansion: There are four main divisions in the Gospel Era:

1. Early Life
2. Early Ministry
3. Later Ministry
4. Death and Resurrection

1. Early Life: Childhood to baptism

Through a miraculous conception by the Holy Spirit, Jesus is born of the Virgin Mary in Bethlehem of Judea. After a brief excursion into Egypt to save Him from Herod's attempt on His life, Jesus travels with Mary and her husband Joseph to live in Nazareth. There He learns the trade of a carpenter and apparently lives a fairly normal life from *childhood to the time of His baptism*, when He is thirty years old. His cousin, John the Baptist, is ministering and baptizing people in the Jordan River near the Dead Sea. After Jesus is baptized by John, a remarkable event takes place. God the Father is heard speaking from heaven, saying, "This is My beloved Son, in whom I am well pleased," and the Holy Spirit, in the visible form of a dove, descends on Him. Then He is led by the Holy Spirit into the wilderness of Judea, where He is tempted by Satan for forty days. Satan makes every attempt to get Jesus to follow him rather than God. Satan offers Jesus everything God the Father offers Him, but on a different timetable and with different requirements. Jesus remains sinless and validates His readiness to begin making Himself known as the Messiah.

2. Early Ministry: Initial acceptance

It is not until after Jesus' baptism and temptation that He begins His public ministry. His message has a two-fold focus. First, He is the predicted Messiah or, as the word is translated in the New Testament, the Christ, and people should believe in Him. Second, He challenges the people to live a life of genuine righteousness, not the external hypocrisy of the religious leaders. He validates His message by performing astounding miracles, and the signs of *initial acceptance* by the crowds are encouraging. Much of this early activity takes place around Jerusalem.

3. Later Ministry: Growing rejection

Jesus' initial popularity does not last. The religious leaders are profoundly jealous of Him and begin stirring up animosity toward Him. This *growing rejection* results in a progression in Jesus' ministry pattern. He begins to focus more attention on the mounting opposition from the religious leaders, warning them of the seriousness of their attitude. At the same time, He begins setting aside more and more time for the twelve disciples whom He has chosen, preparing them to carry on without Him. Also, He begins challenging the multitude to count the cost of following Him. Though Jesus travels quite a bit during this time, His home base is Capernaum, on the north bank of the Sea of Galilee.

4. Death and Resurrection: Final rejection

The Jews become more and more polarized about Jesus, either following Him enthusiastically or resenting Him deeply. In the volatile atmosphere of the festival time of the Passover when Jesus and many other Jews are in Jerusalem, the religious leaders are finally able to stir up enthusiasm for Jesus' crucifixion. They subject Him to a series of mock trials on false charges. Then Jesus is crucified on Friday, buried that night, and rises again from the dead on Sunday, after being in the tomb three days.

SELF-TEST

A. Four Main Divisions in the Gospel Era

(Write in the correct division from the options at left.)

OPTIONS:	DIVISION:	DESCRIPTION:
Early Life	*Early ministry*	Initial acceptance
Early Ministry	*Death Resurrection*	Final rejection
Later Ministry	*Early Life*	Childhood to baptism
Death and Resurrection	*Later ministry*	Growing rejection

B. Story Line Summary

(Fill in the blanks from memory.)

ERA	SUMMARY
Gospel	Jesus comes in fulfillment of the Old Testament _prophecies_ of a savior and offers _Salvation_ and the true kingdom of God. While some accept Him, most _reject_ Him, and He is crucified, buried, and resurrected.

C. Arc of Bible History

(Fill in the names of the eras.)

1. Creation	5. Judges	9. Silence
2. Patriarch	6. Kingdom	10. Gospels
3. Exodus	7. Exile	11. Churche
4. Conquest	8. Return	12. missions

D. The Geography of the Gospel Era

(Draw an arrow from Bethlehem to Egypt to Nazareth to represent the geographical movement in Jesus' early life, and label it 1. Draw an arrow from Nazareth to Jerusalem to represent His initial acceptance, and label it 2. Draw an arrow from Jerusalem to Capernaum to represent the growing rejection, and label it 3. Draw an arrow from Capernaum to Jerusalem to represent His final rejection, and label it 4.)

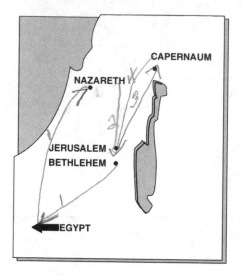

E. Story of the Bible

(Fill in the blanks. To check your answers, see the Appendix.)

ERA	FIGURE		STORY LINE SUMMARY
Creation	Adam	Eden	Adam is created by God, but he _sins_ and _destroys_ God's original _plan_ for man.
Patriarch	Abraham	Canaan	*Abraham* is _chosen_ by God to "father" a _people_ to _represent_ God to the world.
Exodus	Moses	Egypt	Through Moses God _delivers_ the Hebrew people from _slavery_ in Egypt and then gives them the _Law_.
Conquest	Joshua	Canaan	*Joshua* leads the _conquest_ of the _Promised Land_.

ERA	FIGURE		STORY LINE SUMMARY
Judges	_Samson_	_Canaan_	*Samson* and others were chosen as _judges_ to _govern_ the people for _400_ rebellious years.
Kingdom	_David_	_Israel_	*David*, the greatest king in the new _monarchy_, is followed by a succession of mostly _unrighteous_ kings, and God eventually _judges_ Israel for her sin, sending her into exile.
Exile	_Daniel_	_Babylonia_	*Daniel* gives _leadership_ and encourages _faithfulness_ among the _exiles_ for the next seventy years.
Return	_Ezra_	_Jerusalem_	*Ezra* _leads_ the people back from _Exile_ to rebuild _Jerusalem_.
Silence	_Pharisees_	_Jerusalem_	*Pharisees* and others _entomb_ the Israelites in _legalism_ for the next _400_ years.
Gospels	_Jesus_	_Palestine_	*Jesus* comes in fulfillment of the Old Testament _prophecies_ of a savior and offers _salvation_ and the true kingdom of God. While some accept Him, most _reject_ Him, and He is crucified, buried, and resurrected.

CHAPTER SEVENTEEN

THE CHURCH ERA

(ACTS 1—12)

 A LOT OF POTSHOTS HAVE BEEN TAKEN AT THE CHURCH OVER the years. One scalawag wrote:

> To live above with saints we love,
> O, that will be glory.
> To live below with saints we know,
> Well, that's another story.

Another one wrote about hymns we really sing:

> When morning guilds the skies
> My heart awakening cries
> Oh no! Another day!

> Amazing grace, how sweet the sound
> That saved a wretch like you.

> Jesus, I am resting, resting,
> Resting, resting, resting, resting.

> The strife is o'er, the battle done,
> The church has split, and our side won.

William Blake wrote in the "Everlasting Gospel":

> Both read the Bible day and night,
> But Thou read'st black where I read white.

In spite of its obvious imperfections, the church is the means that has been chosen to carry the message of the gospel to the world. One wonders why a better system could not have been devised. Then one realizes that any system that has people in it is going to be imperfect.

Aleksander Solzhenitsyn wrote in the *Gulag Archipelago* that it was in prison where he learned that the line separating good and evil passes not through states, not through classes, not through political parties, either, but right through every human heart.

When we give ourselves serious evaluation, we find things hiding in our hearts that, if we could choose, we would remove. Our hearts have been described as "a zoo of lusts, a bedlam of ambitions, a nursery of fears, a harem of fondled hatreds." Yet the church, by its very nature, must be made up of the likes of us.

However, we are not left to ourselves. God is at work in the lives of all willing people, changing and transforming them into something more than they were.

"Imagine yourself a living house," wrote C.S. Lewis. "God comes in to rebuild that house. At first, perhaps, you can understand what He is doing. He is getting the drains right and stopping the leaks in the roof and so on. But presently He starts knocking the house about in a way that hurts abominably and does not seem to make any sense. What on earth is He up to? The explanation is that He is building quite a different house from the one you thought of—throwing out a new wing here, putting on an extra floor there, running up towers, making courtyards. You thought you were going to be made into a decent little cottage; but He is building a palace."

And thus is the message of the church. The gospel is carried *to* imperfect people *by* imperfect people. Then those imperfect people are to band together to help one another grow to spiritual maturity. Salvation in Christ, and growth to Christian maturity—warts and all.

I. Review: Fill in the blanks to bring the chart up-to-date with this era.

STORY OF THE NEW TESTAMENT

ERA	FIGURE		STORY LINE SUMMARY
Gospels	Jesus	Palestine	*Jesus* comes in fulfillment of the Old Testament prophecies of a savior and offers salvation and the true kingdom of God. While some accept Him, most reject Him, and He is crucified, buried, and resurrected.

ERA	FIGURE		STORY LINE SUMMARY
Church	*Peter*	*Jerusalem*	To be supplied later.

II. Story Line Summary: *Peter,* shortly after the *Ascension* of Jesus, is used by God to *establish* the *church,* God's next major plan for man.

ERA	SUMMARY
Church	*Peter,* shortly after the *Ascension* of Jesus, is used by God to *establish* the *church*, God's next major plan for man.

III. Expansion: There are four major subjects in the Church Era:

1. Creation
2. Growth
3. Persecution
4. Transition

1. Creation: Birth of the church (Acts 1—5)

The birthplace of the church is Jerusalem. After His death, burial, and resurrection, Jesus instructs His disciples to wait in Jerusalem until they receive the power of the Holy Spirit and then to be witnesses to Him in Jerusalem (their city), Judea and Samaria (the surrounding provinces), and the remotest part of the earth (the rest of the world). Then Jesus ascends into heaven right before their eyes. Shortly after that, on the Jewish feast day of Pentecost, the Holy Spirit comes upon Jesus' disciples. While they are gathered in a house, a sound like a violent rushing wind fills the place and flames of fire rest on each disciple, and they are filled with the Holy Spirit. They begin speaking in different foreign languages, with the result that many of the Jews from different parts of the world hear them speak in their own language. This and other notable miracles associated with the *birth of the church* take place in the early days as the number of converts to Christianity increases rapidly in Jerusalem.

2. Growth: Organization of the church (Acts 6)

As the number of converts increases, some measures are taken for the *organization of the church*, giving structure to their activities and responsibilities. Peter organizes a relief effort for needy Christians. Those who have possessions can sell them and give money to the apostles, who distribute it according to the needs. Then deacons are chosen to look after the material needs of the church while the apostles attend to the spiritual needs.

3. Persecution: The first Christian martyr (Acts 7)

Stephen, one of the early preachers, is arrested by the Jewish leaders for preaching about Jesus. When he does not recant his message but presses it further, the Jews stone him to death on the spot, making Stephen *the first Christian martyr*. This incident kicks off a round of persecution against new Christians that is so severe many of them have to flee Jerusalem for their very lives. As they do, they take the message of the gospel with them to the surrounding provinces of Judea and Samaria.

4. Transition: A missionary to the Gentiles (Acts 8—12)

A zealous Pharisee, Saul of Tarsus, looks after the cloaks of those who stone Stephen. Shortly afterward, he is journeying to Damascus to find and persecute other Christians when Jesus appears to him from heaven, and Saul is converted to Christianity. Jesus changes Saul's name to Paul, and he becomes known as the apostle Paul. Jesus expressly tells Paul that he will become *a missionary to the Gentiles.* Shortly after that, the apostle Peter has a vision in which the Lord tells him that the message of the gospel is to be taken to the Gentiles also. This marks a transition in the nature of the Church because, up to this time, the message has been circulated exclusively to Jews.

SELF-TEST

A. Four Major Subjects of the Church Era

(Write in the correct subject from the options at left.)

OPTIONS:	SUBJECT:	DESCRIPTION:
Creation	*Growth*	Organization of the church
Growth	*Transition*	A missionary to the Gentiles
Persecution	*Creation*	Birth of the church
Transition	*Persecution*	The first Christian martyr

B. Story Line Summary

(Fill in the blanks from memory.)

ERA	SUMMARY
Church	*Peter,* shortly after the *Ascension* of Jesus, is used by God to *establish* the *church*, God's next major plan for man.

C. Arc of Bible History *(Fill in the names of the eras.)*

1. C*reation*	5. J*udges*	9. S*ilence*
2. P*atriarch*	6. K*ingdom*	10. G*ospels*
3. E*xodus*	7. E*xile*	11. C*hurch*
4. C*onquest*	8. R*eturn*	12. *missions*

D. The Geography of the Church Era

(Draw an arrow from Jerusalem into Samaria, and one from Jerusalem into Judea to represent the geographical movement of the Church Era.)

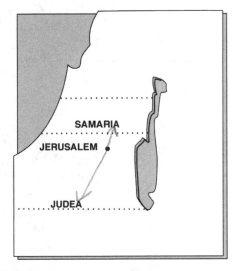

E. Story of the Bible

(Fill in the blanks. To check your answers, see the Appendix.)

ERA	FIGURE		STORY LINE SUMMARY
Creation	Adam	Eden	Adam is created by God, but he ___SiNS___ and ___destroys___ God's original ___plan___ for man.
Patriarch	Abraham	Canaan	*Abraham* is ___chosen___ by God to "father" a ___people___ to ___represent___ God to the world.
Exodus	Moses	Egypt	Through Moses God ___delivers___ the Hebrew people from ___slavery___ in Egypt and then gives them the ___LAW___.
Conquest	Joshua	Canaan	*Joshua* leads the ___conquest___ of the ___Promised Land___.

ERA	FIGURE		STORY LINE SUMMARY
Judges	Samson	Canaan	Samson and others were chosen as _judges_ to _govern_ the people for _400_ rebellious years.
Kingdom	David	Israel	David, the greatest king in the new _monarchy_, is followed by a succession of mostly _unrighteous_ kings, and God eventually _judges_ Israel for her sin, sending her into exile.
Exile	Daniel	Babylonia	Daniel gives _leadership_ and encourages _faithfulness_ among the _exiles_ for the next seventy years.
Return	Ezra	Jerusalem	Ezra _leads_ the people back from _exile_ to rebuild _Jerusalem_.
Silence	Pharisees	Jerusalem	Pharisees and others _entomb_ the Israelites in _legalism_ for the next _400_ years.
Gospels	Jesus	Palestine	Jesus comes in fulfillment of the Old Testament _prophecies_ of a savior and offers _salvation_ and the true kingdom of God. While some accept Him, most _reject_ Him, and He is crucified, buried, and resurrected.
Church	Peter	Jerusalem	Peter, shortly after the _Ascension_ of Jesus, is used by God to _establish_ the _Church_, God's next major plan for man.

CHAPTER EIGHTEEN

THE MISSIONS ERA

(ACTS 13—28)

A MISSIONARY MINISTERING IN THE SOUTH SEA ISLANDS WAS teaching his people about Christmas. "The giving of gifts is a spontaneous act of celebration over an extremely joyous event. And that," he explained, "is why many people give gifts to others at Christmas time. It is an act of celebration over the joyous occasion of the birth of Christ."

Following this teaching, one of the young men wanted to give the missionary a gift for Christmas, but since it was a very poor island, presents were not readily available.

On Christmas morning, a knock came at the hut of the missionary. At the door, he found the young man, who then gave him an extremely rare and particularly beautiful seashell that was found only at the distant end of the island.

The missionary thanked the young man for giving him such a rare and beautiful gift from such a distance, to which the young man replied, "Long walk part of gift."

What a beautiful sentiment. "Long walk part of gift." Such was also true of the apostle Paul, who gave up a life of comfort and safety and took upon himself the arduous life of a missionary to take the message of the gospel to the Gentile people in the surrounding nations.

I. Review: Fill in the blanks to bring the chart up-to-date with this era.

STORY OF THE NEW TESTAMENT

ERA	FIGURE		STORY LINE SUMMARY
Gospels	_Jesus_	_Palestine_	Jesus comes in fulfillment of the Old Testament _prophecies_ of a savior and offers _salvation_ and the true kingdom of God. While some accept Him, most _reject_ Him, and He is crucified, buried, and resurrected.
Church	_Peter_	_Jerusalem_	Peter, shortly after the _Ascension_ of Jesus, is used by God to _establish_ the _Church_, God's next major plan for man.
Missions	_Paul_	_Roman Empire_	To be supplied later.

II. Story Line Summary: Paul _expands_ the church into the _Roman_ Empire during the next two _decades_.

ERA	SUMMARY
Missions	Paul _expands_ the church into the _Roman_ Empire during the next two _decades_.

III. Expansion: There are four major subjects in the Missions Era:

1.   First Missionary Journey

2.   Second Missionary Journey

3.   Third Missionary Journey

4.   Trials and Imprisonment

1. **First Missionary Journey: Galatia for two years**
   (Acts 13—14)

   In Paul's first missionary journey, he and Barnabas are selected by the Holy Spirit to travel to Galatia and take the gospel to Gentiles living there. They depart from Antioch, the point of departure for all three missionary journeys, and are in *Galatia for two years*, experiencing encouraging results. After they return to Jerusalem, a council is held amid much controversy, which determines that the Gentiles do not have to become Jewish in addition to becoming Christians.

2. **Second Missionary Journey: Greece for three years**
   (Acts 15—17)

   Paul leaves from Antioch to visit the believers from his first journey. However, he receives a vision of a man in Macedonia (Greece) and changes his plans, going to Greece with the gospel message for the Gentiles there. He travels in *Greece for three years*.

3. **Third Missionary Journey: Asia for four years**
   (Acts 18—21).

   Again, Paul leaves to encourage the believers from his first two trips and to spread the message of the gospel into Asia. He has great success and great opposition. In Ephesus, the whole city breaks out in riot over his visit. Though Paul is warned that he will be imprisoned upon his return to Jerusalem, he returns anyway, after being in *Asia for four years*, and is immediately arrested.

4. **Trials and Imprisonment: Roman prison for two years**
   (Acts 22—28)

   Jewish leaders in Jerusalem have Paul arrested on false charges. Since his life is threatened there, even under guard, he is moved to Caesarea, the Roman capital in the area. There, he is tried under three men: Felix, Festus, and Agrippa. In order to thwart a miscarriage of justice in the process, Paul exercises his right as a Roman citizen to take his case before Caesar in Rome. He is taken to Rome, but his case never comes to trial. After being in a *Roman prison for two years*, it is said he was beheaded (the established means of execution for a Roman citizen).

SELF-TEST

A. Four Major Subjects of the Missions Era

(Match the missionary journey with its location, choosing from the options at left.)

OPTIONS:	JOURNEY:	LOCATIONS:
First Missionary Journey	*Trials Imprisonment*	Roman prison for two years
Second Missionary Journey	*1st Missionary Journey*	Galatia for two years
Third Missionary Journey	*3rd M journey*	Asia for four years
Trials and Imprisonment	*2 M journey*	Greece for three years

B. Story Line Summary *(Fill in the blanks from memory.)*

ERA	SUMMARY
Missions	Paul _expands_ the church into the _Roman_ Empire during the next two _decades_.

C. Arc of Bible History *(Fill in the names of the eras.)*

1. C_reation_	5. J_udges_	9. S_ilence_
2. P_atriarch_	6. K_ingdom_	10. G_ospels_
3. E_xodus_	7. E_xile_	11. C_hurch_
4. C_onquest_	8. R_eturn_	12. M_issions_

D. The Geography of the Missions Era

(Draw an arrow from Antioch to Galatia and put a 1 next to it. Draw an arrow from Antioch to Greece and put a 2 next to it. Draw an arrow from Antioch to Asia and put a 3 next to it. This represents the geographical movement of Paul's missionary journeys. Now, draw an arrow from Caesarea to Rome and put a 4 next to it to represent Paul's trials and imprisonment during the Missions Era.)

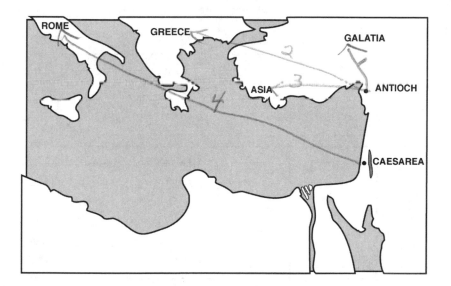

E. Story of the Bible

(Fill in the blanks.)

ERA	FIGURE		STORY LINE SUMMARY
Creation	Adam	Eden	Adam is created by God, but he _sins_ and _destroys_ God's original _plan_ for man.
Patriarch	Abraham	Canaan	Abraham is _chosen_ by God to "father" a _people_ to _represent_ God to the world.

145

ERA	FIGURE		STORY LINE SUMMARY
Exodus	Moses	Egypt	Through Moses God _delivers_ the Hebrew people from _slavery_ in Egypt and then gives them the _LAW_.
Conquest	Joshua	Canaan	Joshua leads the _conquest_ of the _Promised Land_.
Judges	Samson	Canaan	Samson and others were chosen as _judges_ to _govern_ the people for _400_ rebellious years.
Kingdom	David	Israel	David, the greatest king in the new _Monarchy_, is followed by a succession of mostly _unrighteous_ kings, and God eventually _judges_ Israel for her sin, sending her into exile.
Exile	Daniel	Babylonia	Daniel gives _leadership_ and encourages _faithfulness_ among the _exiles_ for the next seventy years.
Return	Ezra	Jerusalem	Ezra _leads_ the people back from _exile_ to rebuild _Jerusalem_
Silence	Pharisees	Jerusalem	Pharisees and others _entomb_ the Israelites in _legalism_ for the next _400_ years.

ERA	FIGURE		STORY LINE SUMMARY
Gospels	Jesus	Palestine	Jesus comes in fulfillment of the Old Testament _prophecies_ of a savior and offers _salvation_ and the true kingdom of God. While some accept Him, most _reject_ Him, and He is crucified, buried, and resurrected.
Church	Peter	Jerusalem	Peter, shortly after the _Ascension_ of Jesus, is used by God to _establish_ the _Church_, God's next major plan for man.
Missions	Paul	Roman Empire	Paul _expands_ the church into the _Roman_ Empire during the next two _decades_

CHAPTER NINETEEN

THE EPISTLES

(ROMANS—REVELATION)

 IN A *READER'S DIGEST* ARTICLE ENTITLED "SEND SOMEONE A Smile," a captivating story is told:

One day shortly after my third child was born I received a note from another young mother, a friend of mine who lived just three blocks from me. We hadn't seen each other all winter.

"Hi, friend," she wrote. "I think of you often. Someday we'll have time to spend together like in the old days. Keep plugging. I know you're a super mother. See you soon, I hope." It was signed: "Your friend on hold, Sue Ann."

The few words lifted my spirits and added a soothing ointment of love to a hectic day. I remember thinking, *Thanks, Sue Ann. I needed that.*

When I went out to mail a note, I noticed a neighbor checking his mailbox. Mr. Williams' head drooped and his pace seemed slower as he shuffled back to his house empty-handed. I hurried back into my own house because I could hear my baby crying, but I couldn't get Mr. Williams off my mind. It wasn't a check he was waiting for; he was quite well-to-do. He was probably looking for some love in his mailbox. While Meagan drew a picture of a mailbox with a smile in it and Tami drew a rainbow, I wrote a little note. "We are your secret admirers," it began. We added a favorite story and a poem. "Expect to hear from us often," I wrote on the envelope.

The next day my children and I watched Mr. Williams take out his mail and open the envelope right in the driveway. Even at a distance, we could see he was smiling.

My mind began reeling when I thought of all the people who could use smiles in their mailboxes. What about the 15-year-old Down's-syndrome girl near my parents whose birthday was coming up? The people in the rest home near our house? The invalid woman in our old neighborhood? The endless people I didn't even know who still believed in courtesy and in doing a good job in stores and offices and restaurants? Even on busy days I could find the time to write at least one note.

Notes can be short, and should be anonymous. At first, I wanted credit for the notes. But now, writing them in secret adds a sense of adventure. It's more fun. I once overheard talk of the Phantom Note Lady. They were discussing me, but they didn't know, and I wasn't telling.

Paul and other writers of the Bible had similar concerns for people they loved. They wrote letters both to church congregations and to individuals to encourage them and to instruct them. In the providence of God, these letters were saved and eventually compiled in the "Epistles" section of the Bible. The Epistles were simply letters.

You will recall that thirteen of the Epistles were written by the apostle Paul while the remaining nine had a number of different authors. The chart in the review section below shows the distinction between the Pauline Epistles and the General Epistles.

I. Review:
STRUCTURE OF THE NEW TESTAMENT

Historical	Pauline	General
Matthew	TO CHURCHES:	Hebrews
Mark	Romans	James
Luke	1 Corinthians	1 Peter
John	2 Corinthians	2 Peter
Acts	Galatians	1 John
	Ephesians	2 John
	Philippians	3 John
	Colossians	Jude
	1 Thessalonians	Revelation
	2 Thessalonians	
	TO INDIVIDUALS:	
	1 Timothy	
	2 Timothy	
	Titus	
	Philemon	

Our history study is now completed. From Matthew through Acts, we stretched out a time line for the history of the New Testament. Some of the Epistles were written during this time line, and some of them were written after the time line ends at the close of the Book of Acts. This makes it a little confusing, and somewhat frustrating, because we wish that the Historical Books told all the history during the time the Epistles were being written. They don't, however, and we are left to piece together what history we can from references in the Epistles.

The following chart shows when the Epistles were written in relationship to the time recorded in the Historical Books. The numbers are the years after Christ's birth. The Gospels cover the time from Christ's birth to His death at approximately age thirty. Acts starts almost immediately after, and records events until about A.D. 60. We see then that Galatians was written during the time of the Book of Acts, A.D. 48 specifically. First and Second Thessalonians were written about A.D. 50, etc. Books in the second section are Pauline Epistles, and the books in the last section are the General Epistles.

TIME LINE OF THE NEW TESTAMENT

Historical Books

Gospel–Acts						post–Acts		
A.D. 0	A.D. 30	A.D. 48	A.D. 50	A.D. 53	A.D. 60	A.D. 62	A.D. 67	A.D. 95

Pauline Epistles

		Galatians	1 Thessalonians 2 Thessalonians	1 Corinthians 2 Corinthians Romans	Ephesians Colossians Philemon Philippians	1 Timothy Titus	2 Timothy	

General Epistles

		James				1 Peter 2 Peter	Hebrews Jude	1 John 2 John 3 John Revelation

II. Overview Summary: The *Epistles* are letters to churches and to individuals to *encourage* them and *instruct* them in the Christian faith.

REVIEW

The *Epistles* are letters to churches and to individuals to *encourage* them and *instruct* them in the Christian faith.

III. Expansion: There are four main topics to be dealt with in studying the Epistles:

1. The Nature of the Epistles
2. Pauline Epistles to Churches
3. Pauline Epistles to Individuals
4. General Epistles

1. The Nature of the Epistles: Doctrine, then duty

Epistles are letters written to churches, individuals, or, in some cases, to the Christian public at large. They deal with specific problems and issues of the day but do so in a way that the information is universal and timeless. The typical pattern is to write a section of doctrinal truth and follow up with the practical implications of that truth. *Doctrine, then duty.* Principle, then practice.

2. Pauline Epistles to Churches: Letters to local churches

Thirteen of the twenty-two Epistles of the New Testament are written by the apostle Paul. Nine of these are *letters to local churches* and are named according to which church they are written.

(As you read the description of the book, notice the words in *italics*. Immediately following the description of each book, the description is repeated with a blank space in place of the *italic* word. Fill in the blank space.)

Romans: heavily doctrinal, with the most complete doctrine of *salvation* by grace through faith in all the Bible.

Romans: heavily doctrinal, with the most complete doctrine of _salvation_ by grace through faith in all the Bible.

1 and 2 Corinthians: heavily practical, dealing with a series of specific *problems* in the Corinthian church.

1 and 2 Corinthians: heavily practical, dealing with a series of specific _problems_ in the Corinthian church.

Galatians: written to some of Paul's first converts, refuting *legalism.* _Galatians is where Paul confronted Peter._

Galatians: written to some of Paul's first converts, refuting _legalism?_

Ephesians: deals with the believer's *position* in Christ and its practical implications.

Ephesians: deals with the believer's _position_ in Christ and its practical implications.

Philippians: a warm letter of *joy* despite trials. _Paul throws in prison & Philippi._

Philippians: a warm letter of _joy_ despite trials.

Colossians: the *preeminence* of Christ is its major theme.

Colossians: the _preeminence_ of Christ is its major theme.

1 and 2 Thessalonians: very personal letters dealing with specific issues in the Thessalonian church, including *prophecy* and *practical* living.

1 and 2 Thessalonians: very personal letters dealing with specific issues in the Thessalonian church, including _prophecy_ and _practical_ living.

3. Pauline Epistles to Individuals: Letters to individuals and pastors.

Four of Paul's letters are written *to individuals and pastors* and are named according to whom they were written.

1 and 2 Timothy: two letters to a young pastor in Ephesus. The first letter *counsels* him on local church issues, and the second *encourages* him to remain strong in the faith in the midst of trials.

1 and 2 Timothy: two letters to a young pastor in Ephesus. The first letter *counsels* him on local church issues, and the second *encourages* him to remain strong in the faith in the midst of trials.

Titus: written to the pastor of the church on the island of Crete, it deals largely with local church issues, including the *qualifications* for church leaders.

Titus: written to the pastor of the church on the island of Crete, it deals largely with local church issues, including the *qualifications* for church leaders.

Philemon: written to a slave owner, it urges lenient treatment of a runaway *slave* who has become a Christian and is returning to his Christian master.

Philemon: written to a slave owner, it urges lenient treatment of a runaway *slave* who has become a Christian and is returning to his Christian master.

4. General Epistles: Letters to the Christian public

Written by various authors, the nine General Epistles are *letters to the Christian public* at large (with the exception of 2 and 3 John). They are usually named according to their authorship.

Hebrews: heavily *doctrinal,* this book draws largely on Old Testament truth in teaching New Testament truth to a Jewish audience.

Hebrews: heavily *doctrinal*, this book draws largely on Old Testament truth in teaching New Testament truth to a Jewish audience.

James: an incisive and practical treatment of the proper out-working of Christian *faith* in everyday life.

James: an incisive and practical treatment of the proper out-working of Christian *faith* in everyday life.

1 and 2 Peter: written to believers scattered throughout Asia and Galatia, it deals with the proper response to *suffering* and opposition.

1 and 2 Peter: written to believers scattered throughout Asia and Galatia, it deals with the proper response to *suffering* and opposition.

1, 2, and 3 John: letters from the apostle John dealing with the *love* of God and its outworking in Christians' lives.

1, 2, and 3 John: letters from the apostle John dealing with the *love* of God and its outworking in Christians' lives.

Jude: a brief but powerful book *warning* against ungodly living.

Jude: a brief but powerful book *warning* against ungodly living.

Revelation: a giant of a book, heavily prophetical, dealing with the nature and chronology of the *end times*.

Revelation: a giant of a book, heavily prophetical, dealing with the nature and chronology of the *end times*.

REVIEW

(Match the correct book with its description.)

1. Pauline Epistles to Churches:

a. Colossians

b. Ephesians

c. Galatians

d. 1, 2 Corinthians

e. Romans

f. 1, 2 Thessalonians

g. Philippians

Romans heavily doctrinal, with the most complete doctrine of *salvation* by grace through faith in all the Bible

1 & 2 Corinthians heavily practical, dealing with a series of specific *problems* in the Corinthian church

Galatians written to some of Paul's first converts, refuting *legalism*

Ephesians deals with the believer's *position* in Christ and its practical implications

Philippians a warm letter of *joy* despite trials

Colossians the *preeminence* of Christ is its major theme

1st and 2nd Thessalonians very personal letters dealing with specific issues in the Thessalonian church, including *prophecy* and *practical* living

2. Pauline Epistles to Individuals:

a. Philemon

b. 1, 2 Timothy

c. Titus

1st and 2nd Timothy two letters to a young pastor in Ephesus. The first letter *counsels* him on local church issues, and the second *encourages* him to remain strong in the faith in the midst of trials

Titus written to the pastor of the church on the island of Crete, it deals largely with local church issues, including the *qualifications* for church leaders

Philemon written to a slave owner, it urges lenient treatment of a run-away slave who has become a Christian and is returning to his Christian master

3. General Epistles:

a. Revelation

b. 1, 2, 3 John

c. Hebrews

d. 1, 2 Peter

e. James

f. Jude

Hebrews heavily *doctrinal*, this book draws largely on Old Testament truth in teaching New Testament truth to a Jewish audience

James an incisive and practical treatment of the proper outworking of Christian *faith* in everyday life

1, 2 Peter written to believers scattered throughout Asia and Galatia, it deals with the proper response to *suffering* and opposition

1, 2, 3 John letters from the apostle John dealing with the *love* of God and its outworking in Christians' lives

Jude a brief but powerful book *warning* against ungodly living

Revelation a giant of a book, heavily prophetical, dealing with the nature and chronology of the *end times*

SELF-TEST

FOUR MAIN DISTINCTIONS TO CONSIDER IN STUDYING THE EPISTLES

(Write in the correct epistles from the options at right.)

OPTIONS:	EPISTLES:	DESCRIPTIONS:
The Nature of the Epistles	*Paul's Epistles to Individuals*	Letters to individuals and pastors
Pauline Epistles to Churches	*Pauline Epistles to Churches*	Letters to local churches
Pauline Epistles to Individuals	*General Epistles*	Letters to the Christian public
General Epistles	*The Nature of the Epistles*	Doctrine, then duty

Congratulations! You have just completed a basic overview of the Story of the Bible, all sixty-six books! From the Historical Books of the Old and New Testaments, you have learned: all the main eras, all the central figures, and the main locations of geography, all tied together with a Story Line Summary of the chronological Story of the Bible. You have also learned where the other books—the Poetical and Prophetical books of the Old Testament and the Epistles of the New Testament—fit into that chronological Story of the Bible.

You are now ready for the next section, which will give you a general overview of the Ten Great Doctrines of the Bible.

SECTION THREE

TEN GREAT DOCTRINES OF THE BIBLE

CHAPTER TWENTY

OVERVIEW OF BIBLE DOCTRINE

 THE BIBLE IS MORE THAN HISTORY. IF YOU WOULD KNOW THE Bible, you must go beyond the historical study of its teachings, and taking that plunge is not easy. One day Harry Cohen, then the head of Columbia Studios in Hollywood, was in a conversation with his brother Jack, who suggested to Harry that they produce a biblical epic. "What do you know about the Bible?" cried Harry. "I'll lay you fifty dollars you don't even know the Lord's Prayer." After a moment's thought, Jack began, "Now I lay me down to sleep . . ." and recited the well-known child's bedtime prayer. Harry pulled fifty dollars out of his pocket. "Well, I'll be!" he said as he handed the money to his brother. "I didn't think you knew it."

There have been so many approaches to mastering the teaching of the Bible, some more successful than others. Menelik II, the emperor of Ethiopia from 1889 until 1913, had one eccentricity. If he felt ill, he was convinced that he had only to eat a few pages of the Bible in order to feel better. This odd behavior did him little harm as long as his literary consumption was kept at a modest level. However, in December 1913 he was recovering from a stroke when he suddenly felt extremely ill. On his instructions the complete book of Kings was torn from the Bible and fed to him, page by page. He died before he finished.

Our approach should be more effective and less painful.

When you add all the authors and all the books of the Bible together, and then boil them down to their irreducible minimum, what does the Bible teach? What subjects does it cover, and what does it say about each subject? When you add Moses, David, Jesus, and Paul together, what did they teach about God, Christ, angels, the future? As you begin to answer these questions, you are trafficking in the subject known as "Bible doctrine."

It is difficult to get two people to agree on all points of doctrine. There is an old Irish prayer that says:

> O Lord, turn the hearts of our enemies.
> And if You can't turn their hearts,
> Then turn their ankles,
> So we can know them by their limp.

There are many people limping, in the eyes of others, over certain doctrinal distinctions. However, there is a basic body of doctrine that nearly all Christians have historically agreed upon. It is that body that we will focus upon in this section.

Depending on how finely you split the hairs, different Bible scholars have come up with different numbers of minimum subjects. For the purpose of our study, we will use ten. The ten great doctrines of the Bible are listed below. Every teaching of the Bible is in a subdivision of one of these doctrines, or subjects.

TEN GREAT DOCTRINES OF THE BIBLE

1. The Bible
2. God
3. Christ
4. Holy Spirit
5. Angels
6. Man
7. Sin
8. Salvation
9. Church
10. Future Things

As you read the following descriptions, note that, to help you remember the doctrine, a symbol has been assigned to each one.

1. **The Bible**, symbolized by a book, deals with the origin and nature of the Scriptures. How did we get them? Are they reliable? Are they the Word of God?

2. **God**, symbolized by the crown of a king, deals with the first person of the Trinity. Who is He? What is He like? And what is our relationship to Him?

3. **Christ**, symbolized by the Lamb of God, deals with Jesus of Nazareth, the second person of the Trinity. Was He a man? Was He God? Is He alive today? Is He coming to earth again?

4. **Holy Spirit**, the third person of the Trinity, is symbolized by a dove. Is He a personal being or the religious equivalent of "school spirit"?

5. **Angels**, symbolized by angel wings and a halo, investigates the reality of the spirit world. What about guardian angels? What about demon possession and Satan worship?

6. **Man**, symbolized by an individual, investigates the origin, nature, and destiny of humanity. Were humans created, or did they evolve? Do they have souls? Does the soul live forever?

7. **Sin**, symbolized by a bite taken out of an apple, deals with the nature of mankind's offense against God.

8. **Salvation,** symbolized by a life-preserver, deals with the afterlife, heaven, hell, and whether or not it is safe to die.

9. **Church**, a body of organized believers, is symbolized by a church building and investigates what the church is in the eyes of God and what its responsibilities are.

10. **Future Things**, symbolized by an hour-glass, looks into biblical prophecy and what the Bible says about future events, the end of the world, and eternity.

REVIEW

(Fill in the blanks from the options at the left.)

OPTIONS:	DOCTRINE:	DESCRIPTION:
√ Salvation	*The Bible*	The origin and nature of the Scriptures
√ Christ	*God*	The first person of the Trinity
√ Future Things	*Christ*	The second person of the Trinity
√ God	*Holy Spirit*	The third person of the Trinity
√ The Bible	*angels*	The spirit world
√ Sin	*Church*	Organized believers

Angels _____*Man*_____ The origin, nature, and destiny of humanity

Man _____*Salvation*_____ The afterlife, heaven, hell

Church _____*Sin*_____ Man's offense against God

Holy Spirit _____*Future Things*_____ Biblical prophecy

To further help you remember these ten great doctrines, notice that the order suggests a logical progression. As you read the descriptions below, write the name of the doctrine next to the corresponding number and symbol on the following chart. By following the numbers and arrows on the chart, you can see the logical progression from one doctrine to the next. This will help you remember the ten great doctrines.

1. **The Bible**
   The Bible is the foundation for what we learn about the other nine subjects, so it is first.

2. **God**
   God is the first member of the Trinity.

3. **Christ**
   Christ is the second member of the Trinity.

4. **Holy Spirit**
   The *Holy Spirit* is the third member of the Trinity.

5. **Angels**
   Angels are lower than God, but higher than man, so are placed between God and man.

6. **Man**
   Man is made in the image of God.

7. **Sin**
   Sin is man's shortcomings in God's eyes.

8. **Salvation**
   Salvation is offered by God to man through faith.

9. **Church**

The *Church* proclaims the message of salvation.

10. **Future Things**

Future Things are a prophetic record of things that will happen in the future.

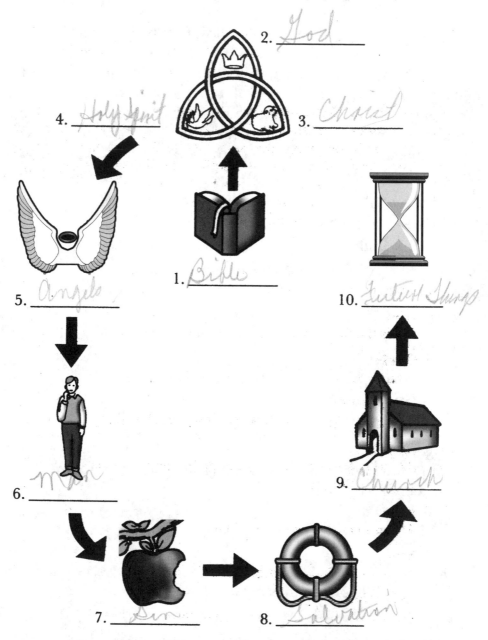

2. God

4. Holy Spirit   3. Christ

1. Bible

5. Angels

10. Future Things

6. man

9. Church

7. Sin

8. Salvation

REVIEW

TEN GREAT DOCTRINES OF THE BIBLE

As a final review, fill in the names of the ten doctrines from memory. See pages 163–164 to check your answers.

1. *Bible*

2. *God*

3. *Christ*

4. *Holy Spirit*

5. *Angels*

6. *Man*

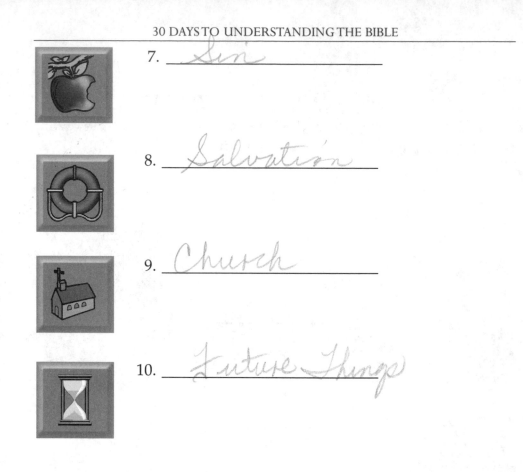

7. ___Sin___

8. ___Salvation___

9. ___Church___

10. ___Future Things___

Now, having established a base of the ten great doctrines of the Bible, we are ready to overview each doctrine separately in the chapters that follow.

CHAPTER TWENTY-ONE

THE DOCTRINE OF THE BIBLE

It is not the things I don't understand about the Bible that bother
me. It's the things I do understand.
—Mark Twain

 LET ME TELL YOU ABOUT THE LAST FLIGHT OF THE *LADY BE Good*, an airplane, a bomber that had seen many successful wartime missions and was out one night on a familiar bombing run. As she flew back toward home base, the crew knew how long it usually took to make the trip.

Tonight, however, there was a powerful tailwind hurtling the massive craft through the air much faster than normal. As the crew plotted their position according to their instruments, they concluded that there must be something wrong with the dials. Their instruments and calculations told them it was time to break down through the cloud layer and land. Their watches and clocks, however, told them this was impossible.

This placed them in a precarious position. If they believed their instruments and came down through the cloud layer too soon, they might be spotted by the enemy and shot down with antiaircraft fire. If they believed their clocks and came down too late, they would overshoot the airfield and perish in the desert beyond.

They chose to ignore the instruments and believe their gut-level hunch. They stayed up. They overshot the airfield and their plane was found days later, crashed in the desert. All the crew had perished.

The story of the *Lady Be Good* is a microcosm of life. We are all on the *Lady Be Good,* and we are all in flight. In making the determination on where and when to land we have to make decisions. And for those decisions we must choose whether we look outside ourselves

. . . whether we trust our gut-level hunches or whether we look for an instrument panel.

The Bible offers itself as the source of truth. The Bible presents itself as the great, cosmic "instrument panel." It tells us where we came from, where we are, and where we are going. It is up to us to decide whether we accept the "readings" we get from it.

The Bible does not defend itself. It was written to people who accepted its message and therefore spends little time convincing its readers of its authenticity. The fundamental assertion that the Bible makes concerning itself is that, in spite of the human collaboration in the writing of it, the Bible is a revelation of God to man, it was written without error, and it can be trusted to reveal truth to us regarding God, man, life, and death.

As we begin our study of the doctrine of the Bible, we will adopt a pattern that will be followed throughout this section:

I.   You will be asked to review the previous chapter.

II. You will then be given an overview of the doctrine, focusing on three things:
   A. The four major subdivisions of each doctrine, assigning a visual symbol to each.
   B. A brief definition for each subdivision, followed by an expansion.
   C. A central Scripture passage for each subdivision.

III. Three of the doctrines will require some additional attention, which will be dealt with under the heading, "Further Considerations."

I. Review: Fill in the blanks. For answers, see pages 165–166.

TEN GREAT DOCTRINES OF THE BIBLE

1. B_ible_

2. G_od_

3. C_hrist_

4. H_Holy Spirit_ S_____

5. A_ngels_

6. M_an_

7. S_in_

8. S_alvation_

9. C_Church_

10. F_uture_ T_hings_

II. The Four Major Subdivisions of the Doctrine of the Bible Are:

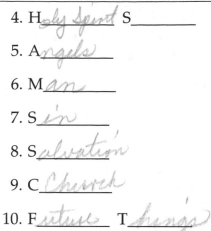
1. Revelation

2. Inspiration

3. Illumination

4. Interpretation

171

(As you read the definitions of the doctrine subdivisions, notice the words in italics. Immediately following the definitions, they are repeated with blank spaces in place of the italic words. Fill in the blank spaces.)

SYMBOL:	SUBDIVISION:	DEFINITION:

1. Revelation: The Bible was *revealed* to man by God.

   Revelation: The Bible was _revealed_ to man by God.

God made known to man that which He wanted man to know. Some of the information related to present-day instruction on how to live and be rightly related to God and one's fellow man. Other information related to prophetic statements about the future. Hebrews 3:7 says, "Therefore, just as the Holy Spirit says. . . ." Then it quotes a passage from Psalms, which was written by King David, indicating that the human writing was *revealed* by God.

CENTRAL PASSAGE:

Therefore, just as the Holy Spirit says, "Today if you hear His voice. . . ." (Hebrews 3:7)

SYMBOL:	SUBDIVISION:	DEFINITION:

2. Inspiration: God saw to it that when men wrote down His revelation, they did so *without error*.

   Inspiration: God saw to it that when men wrote down His revelation, they did so _without error_.

Not all of God's revelation to man was recorded in the Bible. Some of it was very personal, between God and one individual. But for that part of God's revelation to man that was written down, God became involved in the recording process to such a degree that, while He did not dictate or override each individual author's personality, He saw to it that what the writer did record was what He wanted recorded and that it was *without error.*

CENTRAL PASSAGE:

Men moved by the Holy Spirit spoke from God. (2 Peter 1:21)

SYMBOL:	SUBDIVISION:	DEFINITION:

3. Illumination: The Holy Spirit must enable people to *understand* and *embrace* the truth of Scripture.

Illumination: The Holy Spirit must enable people to *understand* and *embrace* the truth of Scripture.

Man's natural ability to grasp and embrace the information in the Bible is limited. Much of it is spiritual information that man does not readily understand or accept. To overcome this fact, the Holy Spirit gradually illumines the receptive mind to *understand* and *embrace* more and more of the Bible, as the Christian matures in his or her spiritual walk.

CENTRAL PASSAGE:

Now we have received, not the spirit of the world, but the Spirit who is from God, that we might know the things freely given to us by God. (1 Corinthians 2:12)

SYMBOL:	SUBDIVISION:	DEFINITION:

4. Interpretation: We must be diligent *students* of Scripture to understand its deeper teachings.

Interpretation: We must be diligent *students* of Scripture to understand its deeper teachings.

Gaining a deeper grasp of the Bible is a two-way street. It is true that it will not happen unless the Holy Spirit illumines the mind of the Christian, but neither will it happen unless the Christian is diligent in pursuing biblical knowledge. The more the Christian reads and studies the Bible, the more the Holy Spirit will illumine his or her mind, which encourages the *student* to read and study further.

CENTRAL PASSAGE:

Be diligent to present yourself approved to God as a workman who does not need to be ashamed, handling accurately the word of truth. (2 Timothy 2:15)

THE DOCTRINE OF THE BIBLE

(Write the titles of the four subdivisions on the lines below.)

SYMBOL:	SUBDIVISION:	DEFINITION:
	1. Revelation	The Bible was *revealed* to man by God.

CENTRAL PASSAGE: Hebrews 3:7

SYMBOL:	SUBDIVISION:	DEFINITION:
	2. Inspiration	GOD SAW TO IT THAT WHEN MEN WROTE DOWN HIS REVELATION, THEY DID SO *WITHOUT ERROR*.

CENTRAL PASSAGE: 2 Peter 1:21

SYMBOL:	SUBDIVISION:	DEFINITION:
	3. Illumination	The Holy Spirit must enable people to *understand* and *embrace* the truth of Scripture.

CENTRAL PASSAGE: 1 Corinthians 2:12

SYMBOL: **SUBDIVISION:** **DEFINITION:**

4. Interpretation   We must be diligent *students* of Scripture to understand its deeper teachings.

CENTRAL PASSAGE: 2 Timothy 2:15

THE DOCTRINE OF THE BIBLE

(Name the four subdivisions of the doctrine of the Bible, and fill in the key words in the definitions.)

SYMBOL: **SUBDIVISION:** **DEFINITION:**

1. Revelation   The Bible was _revealed_ to man by God.

CENTRAL PASSAGE: Hebrews 3:7

SYMBOL: **SUBDIVISION:** **DEFINITION:**

2. Inspiration   God saw to it that when men wrote down His revelation, they did so _without error_.

CENTRAL PASSAGE: 2 Peter 1:21

SYMBOL: **SUBDIVISION:** **DEFINITION:**

3. Illumination   The Holy Spirit must enable people to _understand_ and _embrace_ the truth of Scripture.

CENTRAL PASSAGE: 1 Corinthians 2:12

SYMBOL: **SUBDIVISION:** **DEFINITION:**

4. Interpretation   We must be diligent _students_ of Scripture to understand its deeper teachings.

CENTRAL PASSAGE: 2 Timothy 2:15

SELF-TEST

(Fill in the blanks.)

1. R*evelation* The Bible was ___*revealed*___ to man by God.

2. I*nspiration* God saw to it that when men wrote down His revelation, they did so ___*without*___ ___*error*___.

3. I*llumination* The Holy Spirit must enable people to ___*understand*___ and ___*embrace*___ the truth of Scripture.

4. I*nterpretation* We must be diligent ___*students*___ of Scripture to understand its deeper teachings.

TEN GREAT DOCTRINES OF THE BIBLE

(From memory, fill in the name of doctrine number one. See the Appendix for the answer.)

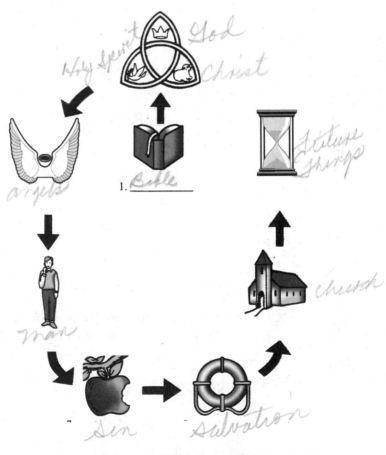

1. *Bible*

CHAPTER TWENTY-TWO

THE DOCTRINE OF GOD

 GOD IS NOT TO BE FOUND IN THE LABORATORY. HE CANNOT BE proved. But then, love is not to be found in the laboratory. Neither is courage, nor longing, nor hope. God is to be found in the courtroom. While data cannot be garnered to prove His existence, evidence can be amassed to demonstrate the probability of His existence. There *is* a gap between the probable and the proved. But then, few things can be proved to the unbelieving mind. Unbelief never has enough proof.

C. S. Lewis, the brilliant Christian scholar who taught at both Cambridge and Oxford, readily admitted his reluctance to accept the existence of God. Yet he kept an open mind in the investigation of the evidence and found himself being convinced in spite of himself. He wrote in his book *Surprised by Joy* that he was teaching at Magdalen College at the University of Oxford when he had an encounter with an atheist intellectual:

> Early in 1926 the hardest boiled of all the atheists I ever knew sat in my room on the other side of the fire and remarked that the evidence for the historicity of the Gospels was really surprisingly good. "Rum thing," he went on. "Rum thing. It almost looks as if it had really happened once." To understand the shattering impact of it, you would need to know the man (who has certainly never since shown any interest in Christianity). If he, the cynic of cynics, the toughest of the toughs, were not—as I would still have put it—"safe," where could I turn? Was there then no escape?
>
> You must picture me alone in that room at Magdalen, night after night, feeling, whenever my mind lifted even for a second from my work, the steady, unrelenting hand of Him whom I so earnestly desired not to meet. That which I greatly feared had at last come upon

me. In the Trinity Term of 1929 I gave in, and admitted that God was God, and knelt and prayed: perhaps, that night, the most dejected and reluctant convert in all England. I did not then see what is now the most shining and obvious thing: the Divine humility which will accept a convert even on such terms. The Prodigal Son at least walked home on his own feet. But who can duly adore the Love which will open the high gates to a prodigal who is brought in kicking, struggling, resentful, and darting his eyes in every direction for a chance of escape?

If you look for God in the laboratory, you will not find Him. If you look for Him in the courtroom, the evidence is conclusive.

I. Review: Fill in the blanks.

THE DOCTRINE OF THE BIBLE

1. R _evelation_
2. I _nspiration_
3. I _llumination_
4. I _nterpretation_

II. The Four Major Subdivisions of the Doctrine of God Are:

1. Existence

2. Attributes

3. Sovereignty

4. Trinity

(As you read the definitions of the doctrine subdivisions, notice the words in italics. Immediately following the definitions, they are repeated with blank spaces in place of the italic words. Fill in the blank spaces.)

SYMBOL: **SUBDIVISION:**   **DEFINITION:**

1. Existence: God *exists.*

   Existence: God _exists_ .

   In a scientific culture, some are reluctant to believe in a being they cannot see, hear, smell, taste, or touch. However, God cannot be dealt with in the laboratory. He must be dealt with in the court-room. It is impossible to generate *proof* of His existence, so we must look for *evidence* of His existence. While the Bible simply assumes that God *exists*, it also provides excellent evidence, so that believing in His existence is an intellectually reasonable thing to do.

   CENTRAL PASSAGE:

   For since the creation of the world His invisible attributes, His eternal power and divine nature, have been clearly seen, being understood through what has been made. (Romans 1:20) _General Revelation_

SYMBOL: **SUBDIVISION:**   **DEFINITION:**

2. Attributes: The fundamental *characteristics* of God.

   Attributes: The fundamental _characteristics_ of God.

   God is a personal being, and as such has individual *characteristics* that distinguish Him from all other beings. These characteristics are called "attributes." Some of His attributes are shared by mankind, since God created man after His personal image. These are called "personal" attributes. He has other characteristics, however, which go beyond man and are true of Him alone. These are the attributes that define "deity" and are called "divine" attributes. We will look more closely at them later.

CENTRAL PASSAGE:

Selected passages to be seen later.

SYMBOL:	SUBDIVISION:	DEFINITION:
	3. Sovereignty:	God can do whatever He *wills*.
	Sovereignty:	God can do whatever He *wills*.

God is all-powerful and has the ability to do whatever He wills. This sovereignty is only exercised in harmony with His goodness, righteousness, and other attributes, and it extends to the entirety of creation for all time. In His sovereignty, He has determined everything that has happened and will happen, and yet has done so in such a way that man has true "volition," or choice. This is one of the mysteries, or "unexplainable" things, of Scripture.

CENTRAL PASSAGE:
For I know that the LORD is great,
And that our Lord is above all gods.
Whatever the LORD pleases, He does,
In heaven and in earth, in the seas and in
all deeps. (Psalm 135:5, 6)

SYMBOL:	SUBDIVISION:	DEFINITION:
	4. Trinity:	God is *three* persons, yet *one*.
	Trinity:	God is __3__ persons, yet __1__.

Another mystery of the Scripture is the Trinity. The Bible says distinctly that there is only one true God (Deuteronomy 6:4). But it also seems to say with equal clarity that there was a man, Jesus Christ, who claimed equality with God the Father, and there is someone called the Holy Spirit who is also equal with God the Father. How do you put that together? Historically, the concept has been termed the "Trinity." There is *one* God who exists in *three* persons. While it is impossible to give an illustration of the Trinity, the evidence remains and has been embraced as a fundamental teaching of Christianity from the beginning.

CENTRAL PASSAGE:

Hear, O Israel! The LORD is our God, the LORD is one! (Deuteronomy 6:4)

The grace of the Lord Jesus Christ, and the love of God, and the fellowship of the Holy Spirit, be with you all. (2 Corinthians 13:14)

THE DOCTRINE OF GOD

(Write the titles of the four subdivisions on the lines below.)

[handwritten: Yaweh used 6,800 times in Old Testament]

[handwritten: Acts 5:3+4]

SYMBOL:	SUBDIVISION:	DEFINITION:
	1. E*xistence*	GOD *EXISTS*.

CENTRAL PASSAGE: Romans 1:20

SYMBOL:	SUBDIVISION:	DEFINITION:
	2. A*ttributes*	The fundamental *characteristics* of God.

CENTRAL PASSAGE: Selected passages.
                    (See pages 183–184)

SYMBOL: **SUBDIVISION:** **DEFINITION:**

3. S*overeignty* God can do whatever He *wills*.

CENTRAL PASSAGE: Psalm 135:5, 6

SYMBOL: **SUBDIVISION:** **DEFINITION:**

4. T*rinity* God is *three* persons, yet *one*.

CENTRAL PASSAGES: Deuteronomy 6:4;
2 Corinthians 13:14

THE DOCTRINE OF GOD

(Name the four subdivisions of the doctrine of God, and fill in the key words in the definitions.)

SYMBOL: **SUBDIVISION:** **DEFINITION:**

1. *Existence* God *exists*.

CENTRAL PASSAGE: Romans 1:20

SYMBOL: **SUBDIVISION:** **DEFINITION:**

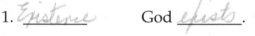

2. *Attributes* The fundamental *characteristics* _____ of God.

CENTRAL PASSAGE: Selected passages.
(See pages 183–184)

SYMBOL: **SUBDIVISION:** **DEFINITION:**

3. *Sovereignty* God can do whatever He *wills*.

CENTRAL PASSAGE: Psalm 135:5, 6

SYMBOL: **SUBDIVISION:** **DEFINITION:**

4. *Trinity* God is __*3*__ persons, yet __*1*__.

CENTRAL PASSAGES: Deuteronomy 6:4;
2 Corinthians 13:14

SELF-TEST

(Fill in the blanks.)

1. E*xistence*   God *exists*.

2. A*ttributes*   The fundamental *characteristics* _____ of God.

3. S*overeignty*   God can do whatever He *wills*.

4. T*rinity*   God is __*3*__ persons, yet __*1*__.

III. Further Consideration of the Attributes of God

The attributes of God require further consideration. While God has many attributes, or characteristics, we will focus on six primary attributes. Three are divine attributes, and three are personal attributes.

A. Divine Attributes

1. Omnipotence: God is all-*powerful.*

   CENTRAL PASSAGE:

   I know that Thou canst do all things, And that no purpose of Thine can be thwarted. (Job 42:2 KJV)

2. Omnipresence: God is *present* everywhere simultaneously.

   CENTRAL PASSAGE:
   If I ascend to heaven, Thou art there;
   If I make my bed in Sheol, behold, Thou art there.
   (Psalm 139:8 KJV)

3. Omniscience: God *knows* all things.

   CENTRAL PASSAGE:
   Even before there is a word on my tongue,
   Behold, O LORD, Thou dost know it all. (Psalm 139:4 KJV)

Review: Divine Attributes
1. Omnipotence: God is all-*powerful.* (Job 42:2)

2. Omnipresence: God is _present_ everywhere simultaneously. (Psalm 139:8)

3. Omniscience: God _knows_ all things. (Psalm 139:4)

B. Personal Attributes

1. Holiness: God is *without evil* and is only good.

                    CENTRAL PASSAGE: Isaiah 5:16

2. Love: God seeks the *best* for *others*.

                    CENTRAL PASSAGE: 1 John 4:8

3. Justice: God applies righteous *consequences* equally to everyone.

                    CENTRAL PASSAGE: Psalm 19:9

Review: Personal Attributes

1. Holiness: God is _without_ _evil_ and is only good. (Isaiah 5:16)

2. Love: God seeks the _best_ for _them_. (1 John 4:8)

3. Justice: God applies righteous _consequences_ equally to everyone. (Psalm 19:9)

SELF-TEST

A. Match the six attributes of God with their definitions by writing the correct letter in the blank.

F Omnipotence _Love_   A. God seeks the *best* for *others*.

D Omnipresence _Justice_   B. God applies righteous *consequences* equally to everyone.

E Omniscience _Holiness_   C. God is *without evil* and is only good.

C Holiness _Omnipresence_   D. God is pesent everywhere simultaneously.

A Love _Omniscience_   E. God knows all things.

B Justice _Omnipotence_   F. God is all-*powerful*.

B. Fill in the blanks.

God's three divine attributes are:
1. _omnipotence_
2. _Omnipresence_
3. _Omniscience_

God's three personal attributes are:
1. _Holiness_
2. _Love_
3. _Justice_

It is worth repeating that there are many more characteristics of God than these. These six were chosen because they were among the most striking and well-known attributes.

TEN GREAT DOCTRINES OF THE BIBLE

(From memory, fill in the names of doctrines one and two. See the Appendix for answers.)

2. Trinity

1. Bible

Deity

God

Holy Spirit

Christ

Angels

Man

Sin

Salvation

Future Things

Church

CHAPTER TWENTY-THREE

THE DOCTRINE OF CHRIST

 ATTITUDES ABOUT JESUS ARE VARIED AND OFTEN ARE STRONGLY held. From denying that a person named Jesus of Nazareth ever existed to believing that He was God incarnate, people demonstrate their conviction about Him by ignoring Him or worshiping Him.

Perhaps the most popular concept of Jesus is that, while He was not divine, He was a great moral teacher and leader. While He is no more God than you or I, He is a wonderful example to follow.

This is a difficult concept to hold consistently. The reason is expressed skillfully by C. S. Lewis, who wrote in his book *Mere Christianity*:

> That is the thing we must not say. A man who was merely a man and said the sort of things that Jesus said would not be a great moral teacher. He would either be a lunatic on the level of a man who says he is a poached egg—or else he would be the devil of hell. You must make your choice. Either this man was, and is, the son of God; or else a madman or something worse. You can shut Him up for a fool, you can spit at Him and kill Him as a demon; or you can fall at His feet and call Him Lord and God. But let us not come with any patronizing nonsense about His being a great human teacher. He has not left that open to us. He did not intend to.

The position of the Bible is straightforward in presenting Jesus as divine, the Son of God, the second person of the Trinity. He is fully man and fully God. If He were not man, He could not have died for our sins, and if He were not God, His death would have accomplished nothing.

To understand the Bible's position on Jesus, it must be grasped that Jesus is presented as the Messiah, the Savior of the world who was prophesied throughout the Old Testament, who would come to die for the sins of the world and who would come again to establish righteousness in a new heaven and new earth.

I. **Review:** Fill in the blanks.

THE DOCTRINE OF THE BIBLE

1. R *evelation*
2. I *nspiration*
3. I *llumination*
4. I *nterpretation*

THE DOCTRINE OF GOD

1. E *xistence*
2. A *ttributes*
3. S *overeignty*
4. T *rinity*

II. The Four Major Subdivisions of the Doctrine of Christ Are:

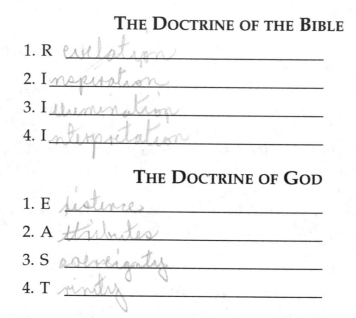

1. Deity

2. Humanity

3. Resurrection

 4. Return

(As you read the definitions of the doctrine subdivisions, notice the words in italics. Immediately following the definitions, they are repeated with blank spaces in place of the italic words. Fill in the blank spaces.)

SYMBOL:	SUBDIVISION:	DEFINITION:
	1. Deity:	Jesus of Nazareth was *God* incarnate.
	Deity:	Jesus of Nazareth was _God_ incarnate.

Though Jesus was man, He was also *God*. The second member of the Trinity existed before He was born as Jesus of Nazareth. Christ was active in the creation of the world and during the Old Testament. When the timing was right, the Christ, the second person of the Trinity, became incarnate as Jesus of Nazareth but did not forfeit His divinity at any time.

CENTRAL PASSAGE:

In the beginning was the Word, and the Word was with God, and the Word was God. (John 1:1)

SYMBOL:	SUBDIVISION:	DEFINITION:

2. Humanity: Christ was a *man,* Jesus of Nazareth.

Humanity: Christ was a _*man*_ , Jesus of Nazareth.

Though Jesus was God, He was also a *man.* Christ took on the form of humanity, and although He did not sin He tasted all other human experiences, including hunger, fatigue, and sorrow, etc. He was supernaturally conceived, was born of a virgin, and lived an apparently normal early life as a carpenter's son in Nazareth of Galilee. As a man, He was crucified, died, and was buried.

CENTRAL PASSAGE:

And the Word became flesh, and dwelt among us, and we beheld His glory, glory as of the only begotten from the Father, full of grace and truth. (John 1:14)

SYMBOL:	SUBDIVISION:	DEFINITION:

3. Resurrection: After being killed, Jesus was *raised* to life again.

Resurrection: After being killed, Jesus was _raised_ to life again.

After being falsely accused and tried in a series of kangaroo courts, Jesus was subjected to the form of capital punishment reserved for non-Roman citizens. He was flogged, a savage punishment which killed 60 percent of its victims; then He was nailed to a wooden cross where He died. Afterward, He was wrapped in burial cloths and placed in a sealed tomb where He remained for three days. At the end of that time, a miraculous earthquake moved the stone from the mouth of the tomb to reveal that Jesus was *raised* from the dead after three days, just as He had said He would be.

CENTRAL PASSAGE:

Who was declared the Son of God with power by the resurrection from the dead, according to the Spirit of holiness, Jesus Christ our Lord. (Romans 1:4)

SYMBOL:	SUBDIVISION:	DEFINITION:
	4. Return:	Jesus will *return* to earth at some time in the future.
	Return:	Jesus will _return_ to earth at some time in the future.

The picture of the Messiah in the Old Testament was an uncertain one. Some of the prophetic passages spoke of a humble-servant Messiah, while other passages spoke of a glorious and powerful king. So stark was the contrast between these two kinds of passages that some Old Testament scholars thought there would be two Messiahs. With the additional revelation in the New Testament, we now know how to reconcile these passages. Jesus came the first time as a humble servant and died for the sins of mankind. After He was resurrected, He ascended into heaven to sit at the right hand of God the Father. Some day in the future, and according to biblical prophecy it could be soon, Jesus will *return* to earth as a powerful and glorious king to institute righteousness on the earth.

CENTRAL PASSAGE:

Looking for the blessed hope and the appearing of the glory of our great God and Savior, Christ Jesus. (Titus 2:13)

THE DOCTRINE OF CHRIST

(Write the titles of the four subdivisions on the lines below.)

SYMBOL:

SUBDIVISION:

DEFINITION:

1. D_eity_   Jesus of Nazareth was *God* incarnate.

CENTRAL PASSAGE: John 1:1

SYMBOL:

SUBDIVISION:

DEFINITION:

2. H_umanity_   Christ was a *man*, Jesus of Nazareth.

CENTRAL PASSAGE: John 1:14

SYMBOL:

SUBDIVISION:

DEFINITION:

3. R_esurrection_   After being killed, Jesus was *raised* to life again.

CENTRAL PASSAGE: Romans 1:4

SYMBOL:

SUBDIVISION:

DEFINITION:

4. R_eturn_   Jesus will *return* to earth at some time in the future.

CENTRAL PASSAGE: Titus 2:13

THE DOCTRINE OF CHRIST

(Name the four subdivisions of the doctrine of Christ and fill in the key words in the definitions.)

SYMBOL:

SUBDIVISION:

DEFINITION:

1. _Deity_   Jesus of Nazareth was _God_ incarnate.

CENTRAL PASSAGE: John 1:1

SYMBOL:

SUBDIVISION:

2. *Humanity*

DEFINITION:

Christ was a ___*man*___, Jesus of Nazareth.

CENTRAL PASSAGE: John 1:14

SYMBOL:

SUBDIVISION:

3. *Resurrection*

DEFINITION:

After being killed, Jesus was *raised* to life again.

CENTRAL PASSAGE: Romans 1:4

SYMBOL:

SUBDIVISION:

4. *Return*

DEFINITION:

Jesus will ___*return*___ to earth at some time in the future.

CENTRAL PASSAGE: Titus 2:13

SELF-TEST

(Fill in the blanks.)

1. D*eity* ___ Jesus of Nazareth was ___*God*___ incarnate.

2. H*umanity* Christ was a ___*man*___, Jesus of Nazareth.

3. R*esurrection* After being killed, Jesus was *raised* to life again.

4. R*eturn* Jesus will ___*return*___ to earth at some time in the future.

TEN GREAT DOCTRINES OF THE BIBLE

(From memory, fill in the names of doctrines one through three. See the Appendix for answers.)

2. _God_

3. _Christ_

1. _Bible_

Angels

man

Sin

Salvation

Future Things

Church

Chapter Twenty-Four

The Doctrine of the Holy Spirit

 THE IRS HAS A "CONSCIENCE FUND" THAT RECEIVES ANONY-mous contributions from people who have cheated the government out of money in the past and who want to make up for it to clear their conscience but don't want to risk criminal prosecution. The Conscience Fund received a check from a man who included the following note:

> I have not been able to sleep ever since I cheated you out of some money, so here is a check for $500. If I still can't sleep, I'll send you the rest.

In another example, a salesman called on a successful contractor with a bid for the materials for a large job the contractor was about to begin. He was invited into the contractor's office, where they chatted for a moment before a secretary came and summoned the contractor into another office. Alone, the salesman noticed that there was a bid from a competitor's firm on the contractor's desk with all the numbers written clearly. The total amount of the bid was hidden, however, covered by a small orange juice can. Unable to contain his curiosity, the salesman picked up the orange juice can. When he did, thousands of BB's came pouring from the bottom of the can which had been cut out, flooded over the surface of the desk, and rained down on the floor. Without saying a word, the salesman turned, walked out of the office, and never returned.

We laugh at the first story and cringe at the second, because we see ourselves in both of them. We all have shortcomings and weakness. We all want to be more than we are. But we need help. Sometimes we need information. Sometimes we need assistance. Sometimes, we need to be challenged or confronted to change. This is a primary role of the Holy Spirit, to work with us in a mystical sort of way to become Christians and then to grow as Christians. He transforms us from what we were like in the past to what we should be like in the future. He is a friend, indeed, because He knows all about us and loves us anyway. He commits Himself to us to help us change, to be the sort of man or woman we long to be deep down in our souls.

I. **Review:** Fill in the blanks.

THE DOCTRINE OF THE BIBLE

1. R _evelation_
2. I _nspiration_
3. I _llumination_
4. I _nterpretation_

THE DOCTRINE OF GOD

1. E _xistence_
2. A _ttributes_
3. S _overeignty_
4. T _rinity_

THE DOCTRINE OF CHRIST

1. D _eity_
2. H _umanity_
3. R _esurrection_
4. R _eturn_

II. **The Four Major Subdivisions of the Doctrine of the Holy Spirit Are:**

1. Personality

2. Deity

3. Salvation

4. Gifts

(As you read the definitions of the doctrine subdivisions, notice the words in italics. Immediately following the definitions, they are repeated with blank spaces in place of the italic words. Fill in the blank spaces.)

SYMBOL:	SUBDIVISION:	DEFINITION:
	1. Personality:	The Holy Spirit is a *personal* being, not an impersonal force.
	Personality:	The Holy Spirit is a _____ being, not an impersonal force.

The Holy Spirit is sometimes perceived as the religious equivalent of school spirit. This is not accurate. In the Bible, the Holy Spirit is treated as a person and given the attributes of *personality*, such as emotions, actions, intellect, and relationships.

CENTRAL PASSAGE:

And do not grieve the Holy Spirit of God, by whom you were sealed for the day of redemption. (Ephesians 4:30)

SYMBOL:	SUBDIVISION:	DEFINITION:

2. Deity: — The Holy Spirit is *divine*, the third person of the Trinity.

Deity: — The Holy Spirit is _divine_, the third person of the Trinity.

Not only is the Holy Spirit a personal being, He is also *divine.* He possesses divine attributes, such as omnipresence and omnipotence. He performed miracles only God could do, such as the creation of the world and the miraculous conception of Jesus. In addition, He is associated on an equal plane with the other members of the Trinity.

CENTRAL PASSAGE:

The grace of the Lord Jesus Christ, and the love of God, and the fellowship of the Holy Spirit, be with you all. (2 Corinthians 13:14)

SYMBOL:	SUBDIVISION:	DEFINITION:

3. Salvation: — The Holy Spirit is *instrumental* in personal salvation.

Salvation: — The Holy Spirit is _instrumental_ in personal salvation.

The Holy Spirit plays the *instrumental* role in the personal salvation of individuals who become Christians. It is the Holy Spirit who enables us to see our sinfulness and realize that we should turn from sin. It is the Holy Spirit who helps us see that, in order to become Christians, we must believe in Jesus, ask Him to forgive us of our sins and give us eternal life, and commit our lives to living for Him.

CENTRAL PASSAGE:

Selected passages to be seen later.

(Note: The significance of the two baby cribs lies in an acrostic. There are five primary areas of involvement by the Holy Spirit in personal salvation: conviction, regeneration, indwelling, baptism, and sealing. The first letters from each of these words spell "CRIBS." We will study the CRIBS concept in more detail later.)

SYMBOL:	SUBDIVISION:	DEFINITION:
	4. Gifts:	The Holy Spirit imparts *spiritual* abilities to Christians.
	Gifts:	The Holy Spirit imparts ~~spiritual~~ abilities to Christians.

God wants to use each of us to minister to others. The Holy Spirit gives us a special *spiritual* "gift" to minister to others. It is something we enjoy doing and something at which we are effective. However, since God is working through us with this gift, the results must always be attributed to Him and not to ourselves. We must guard against two imbalances. We must not become discouraged if our results are meager, and we must not become inflated if our results are abundant. For in the true exercise of spiritual gifts, it is God who produces the results, whether meager or abundant.

CENTRAL PASSAGE:

Now there are varieties of gifts, but the same Spirit. . . . But one and the same Spirit works all these things, distributing to each one individually just as He wills. (1 Corinthians 12:4, 11)

THE DOCTRINE OF THE HOLY SPIRIT

(Write the titles of the four subdivisions on the lines.)

SYMBOL: **SUBDIVISION:** **DEFINITION:**

1. P~~ersonality~~ The Holy Spirit is a *personal* being, not an impersonal force.

CENTRAL PASSAGE: Ephesians 4:30

SYMBOL: **SUBDIVISION:** **DEFINITION:**

2. D~~eity~~ The Holy Spirit is *divine,* the third person of the Trinity.

CENTRAL PASSAGE: 2 Corinthians 13:14

SYMBOL: **SUBDIVISION:** **DEFINITION:**

3. S~~alvation~~ The Holy Spirit is *instrumental* in personal salvation.

CENTRAL PASSAGE: Selected passages.
(See pages 201–203)

SYMBOL: **SUBDIVISION:** **DEFINITION:**

4. G~~ifts~~ The Holy Spirit imparts *spiritual* abilities to Christians.

CENTRAL PASSAGE: 1 Corinthians 12:4, 11

THE DOCTRINE OF THE HOLY SPIRIT

(Name the four subdivisions of the doctrine of the Holy Spirit and fill in the key words in the definitions.)

SYMBOL: **SUBDIVISION:** **DEFINITION:**

1. ~~Personality~~ The Holy Spirit is a ~~personal~~ being, not an impersonal force.

CENTRAL PASSAGE: Ephesians 4:30

SYMBOL: **SUBDIVISION:** **DEFINITION:**

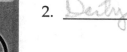

2. ~~Deity~~ The Holy Spirit is ~~divine~~, the third person of the Trinity.

CENTRAL PASSAGE: 2 Corinthians 13:14

SYMBOL:	**SUBDIVISION:**	**DEFINITION:**
	3. _Salvation_	The Holy Spirit is _instrumental_ in personal salvation.

CENTRAL PASSAGE: Selected passages.
(See pages 201–203)

SYMBOL:	**SUBDIVISION:**	**DEFINITION:**
	4. _Gifts_	The Holy Spirit imparts _spiritual_ abilities to Christians.

CENTRAL PASSAGE: 1 Corinthians 12:4, 11

SELF-TEST

(Fill in the blanks.)

1. P_ersonality_   The Holy Spirit is a _personal_ being, not an impersonal force.

2. D_eity_   The Holy Spirit is _divine_, the third person of the Trinity.

3. S_alvation_   The Holy Spirit is _instrumental_ in personal salvation.

4. G_ifts_   The Holy Spirit imparts _spiritual_ abilities to Christians.

III. Further Consideration of the Holy Spirit's Work in Salvation

The work of the Holy Spirit in personal salvation requires further consideration. There are five primary areas of involvement.

1. Conviction: Revealing a *need* to *change*.

    The Holy Spirit convinces a person of his or her *need* to *change* some thought, attitude, or action. This phenomenon is sometimes accompanied by an acute sense of guilt over wrongdoing.

    CENTRAL PASSAGE:

And He [the Holy Spirit], when He comes, will convict the world concerning sin, and righteousness, and judgment. (John 16:8)

2. Regeneration: Imparting a new spirit and *eternal life* with God.

According to the Bible, everyone lives forever, either with God in heaven or separated from Him in hell. When a person becomes a Christian, the Holy Spirit imparts to him or her a new spirit and *eternal life* with God in heaven.

CENTRAL PASSAGE:

He saved us, not on the basis of deeds which we have done in righteousness, but according to His mercy, by the washing of regeneration and renewing by the Holy Spirit. (Titus 3:5)

3. Indwelling: Living *within* a believer.

The Holy Spirit mysteriously "takes up residence" *within* a person when the person becomes a believer, encouraging and strengthening him or her to live a proper lifestyle.

CENTRAL PASSAGE:

You are not in the flesh but in the Spirit, if indeed the Spirit of God dwells in you. But if anyone does not have the Spirit of Christ, he does not belong to Him. (Romans 8:9)

4. Baptism: *Placing* a believer, spiritually, in the body of Christ.

The "body of Christ" is a term given to the totality of all believers in Him. To *baptize* means to "place into." Technically, to be baptized into the body of Christ means to be a member of that spiritual organism.

CENTRAL PASSAGE:

For by one Spirit we were all baptized into one body, whether Jews or Greeks, whether slaves or free, and we were all made to drink of one Spirit. (1 Corinthians 12:13)

5. Sealing: *Guaranteeing* the believer's relationship to God.

The Holy Spirit becomes the *guarantee* of our spiritual inheritance, to be fully realized when we die. This means once a person has been regenerated, indwelt, and baptized into the body of Christ, his or her position is secure, "sealed with the Holy Spirit of promise" until the day of redemption. (Ephesians 1:13)

CENTRAL PASSAGE:

In Him [Christ] you also trusted, after you heard the word of truth, the gospel of your salvation; in whom also, having believed, you were sealed with the Holy Spirit of promise. (Ephesians 1:13, 14 NKJV)

SELF-TEST

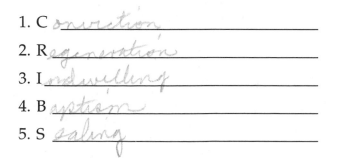

A. The five works of the Holy Spirit in personal salvation are:

1. C onviction
2. R egeneration
3. I ndwelling
4. B aptism
5. S ealing

B. Match the term with the definition by writing the correct letter in the blank.

C Conviction *Regeneration*

A Regeneration *Sealing*

D Indwelling *Conviction*

E Baptism *Indwelling*

B Sealing *Baptism*

A. Imparting a new spirit and *eternal life* with God.

B. *Guaranteeing* the believer's relationship to God.

C. Revealing a *need* to *change*.

D. Living *within* a believer.

E. *Placing* a believer, spiritually, in the body of Christ.

TEN GREAT DOCTRINES OF THE BIBLE

(From memory, fill in the names of doctrines one through four. See the Appendix for answers.)

2. *God*

4. *Holy Spirit*

3. *Christ*

1. *Bible*

angels

man

Future Things

Church

Sin

Salvation

CHAPTER TWENTY-FIVE

THE DOCTRINE OF ANGELS

 IN HIS BOOK ENTITLED *ANGELS*, BILLY GRAHAM TELLS THE story of Dr. S. W. Mitchell, a well-known Philadelphia neurologist, who was awakened from sleep one rainy night by a little girl, poorly dressed and very upset. She said her mother was very sick, and would he come right away. He followed the girl and found the mother desperately ill with pneumonia. After attending her and arranging for medical care, he complimented the sick woman on the intelligence and persistence of her little daughter. As *Reader's Digest* reported in the original story, the woman looked at Dr. Mitchell strangely and said, "My daughter died a month ago." She added, "Her shoes and coat are in the closet there." Puzzled, Dr. Mitchell went to the closet and opened the door. There hung the very coat worn by the little girl who had brought him to care for her mother. It was warm and dry and could not possibly have been out in the inclement weather.

Might the "little girl" have been an angel, sent to aid the stricken mother?

Mr. Graham also tells the story of John G. Paton, a missionary in the New Hebrides Islands. One evening, natives surrounded the missionary compound with the intent of burning down the compound and killing Mr. Paton and his wife. The missionaries prayed fervently all night and were surprised and relieved to witness the natives leaving the next morning.

A year later, the chief of the hostile tribe was converted to Christianity. He told the Patons that he and his tribe had fully intended to destroy the compound and kill the Patons that fateful night a year ago but had been stopped by the army of men surrounding the compound. "Who were all those men you had with you there?" the chief asked. "There were no men there; just my wife and I," replied Mr. Paton. The chief argued that they had seen many men standing guard—hundreds of big men in shining garments with drawn swords in their hands. They seemed to circle the mission station so that the natives were afraid to attack.

Again, angels?

When the brilliant scholar Mortimer Adler undertook to edit *Great Books of the Western World* for the Encyclopedia Britannica Company, he included "Angels" as one of the great themes. Personally curious, Mr. Adler went on to write a book on angels, and in doing so, discovered that from before Aristotle's time to the present day, scholars and philosophers have taken angels seriously.

It is difficult to prove the existence and work of angels. They are not usually perceived by our five senses and are therefore not subject to scientific scrutiny. Nevertheless, they are found throughout the Bible, interwoven into many of the major events of Scripture.

I. **Review:** Fill in the blanks.

THE DOCTRINE OF THE BIBLE

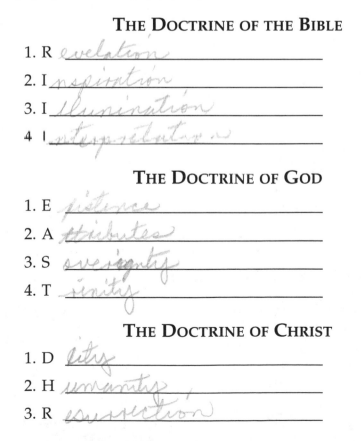

1. R *evelation*
2. I *nspiration*
3. I *llumination*
4. I *nterpretation*

THE DOCTRINE OF GOD

1. E *xistence*
2. A *ttributes*
3. S *overeignty*
4. T *rinity*

THE DOCTRINE OF CHRIST

1. D *eity*
2. H *umanity*
3. R *esurrection*

4. R _Return_

THE DOCTRINE OF THE HOLY SPIRIT

1. P _ersonality_
2. D _eity_
3. S _alvation_
4. G _ifts_

II. The Four Major Subdivisions of the Doctrine of Angels are:

1. Angels

2. Demons

3. Satan

4. Defenses

Conviction C
Indwelling I
Baptism B S

(As you read the definitions of the doctrine subdivisions, notice the words in italics. Immediately following the definitions, they are repeated with blank spaces in place of the italic words. Fill in the blank spaces.)

SYMBOL:	SUBDIVISION:	DEFINITION:

1. Angels: Ministering spirits *from* God.

   Angels: Ministering _from_ from God.

The Bible teaches that God uses a numberless army of angels to help execute His will in heaven and earth, and that among their duties is ministering to Christians. Perhaps this is where the concept of guardian angels came from. They are personal beings, *spirits* that God created before Adam and Eve, and are not "ghosts" of people who have died.

CENTRAL PASSAGE:

Are they [angels] not all ministering spirits, sent out to render service for the sake of those who will inherit salvation? (Hebrews 1:14)

SYMBOL:	SUBDIVISION:	DEFINITION:

2. Demons: Angels who *fell*.

   Demons: Angels who _fell_ .

The Bible teaches that a large number of the "righteous angels" rebelled against God and now form an evil army under the command of the devil, who uses them to further his will, which is counter to the will of God. This corruption is often referred to as the "*fall* " of these angels.

CENTRAL PASSAGE:

And the angels who did not keep their proper domain, but left their own abode, He has reserved in everlasting chains under darkness for the judgment of the great day. (Jude 6 NKJV)

SYMBOL:	SUBDIVISION:	DEFINITION:

3. Satan: The highest angel who *fell*.

Satan: The highest angel who _fell_ .

The Bible teaches that Satan was originally the highest angel, but because of pride he *fell*, rebelling against God and leading many lesser angels to rebel against Him also. In doing this he became evil and corrupt. He is a real entity who oversees the forces of darkness in the world and seeks to neutralize and overthrow the will of God.

CENTRAL PASSAGE:

Be sober, be vigilant; because your adversary the devil walks about like a roaring lion, seeking whom he may devour. (1 Peter 5:8 NKJV)

SYMBOL:	SUBDIVISION:	DEFINITION:

4. Defenses: Using God's *protection*.

Defenses: Using God's _protection_ .

In the Bible, Satan is called the *deceiver* and the *destroyer.* He deceives in order to destroy. A primary strategy is to make that which is wrong look right and that which is right look wrong. The Bible teaches that *protection* from Satan is available to the Christian. These spiritual defenses will be dealt with in greater detail later.

CENTRAL PASSAGE:

Selected passages to be seen later.

THE DOCTRINE OF ANGELS

(Write the titles of the four subdivisions on the lines below.)

| SYMBOL: | SUBDIVISION: | DEFINITION: |

1. A_ngels_   Ministering *spirits* from God.

CENTRAL PASSAGE: Hebrews 1:14

| SYMBOL: | SUBDIVISION: | DEFINITION: |

2. D_emons_   Angels who *fell*.

CENTRAL PASSAGE: Jude 6

| SYMBOL: | SUBDIVISION: | DEFINITION: |

3. S_atan_   The highest angel who *fell*.

CENTRAL PASSAGE: 1 Peter 5:8

| SYMBOL: | SUBDIVISION: | DEFINITION: |

4. D_efense_   Using God's *protection*.

CENTRAL PASSAGE: Selected passages. (See page 213)

THE DOCTRINE OF ANGELS

(Name the four subdivisions of the doctrine of angels and fill in the key words in the definitions.)

SYMBOL: **SUBDIVISION:**   **DEFINITION:**

 1. *Angels*   Ministering *spirits* from God.

CENTRAL PASSAGE: Hebrews 1:14

SYMBOL: **SUBDIVISION:**   **DEFINITION:**

 2. *Demons*   Angels who *fell*.

CENTRAL PASSAGE: Jude 6

SYMBOL: **SUBDIVISION:**   **DEFINITION:**

 3. *Satan*   The highest angel who *fell*.

CENTRAL PASSAGE: 1 Peter 5:8

SYMBOL: **SUBDIVISION:**   **DEFINITION:**

 4. *Defenses*   Using God's *Protection*.

CENTRAL PASSAGE: Selected passages. (See page 213)

SELF-TEST

(Fill in the blanks.)

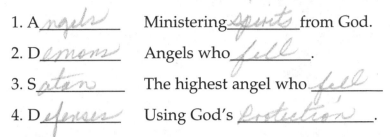

1. A*ngels*   Ministering *spirits* from God.

2. D*emons*   Angels who *fell*.

3. S*atan*   The highest angel who *fell*

4. D*efenses*   Using God's *protection*.

III. Further Consideration of the Believer's Defenses

The believer's defenses against the efforts of Satan to deceive and destroy him or her require further consideration. There are three primary facets to the believer's defense system.

1. Alertness: The Christian must know Satan's intention and be *alert* to his advances.

    CENTRAL PASSAGE:

    Be sober, be vigilant; because your adversary the devil walks about like a roaring lion, seeking whom he may devour. (1 Peter 5:8 NKJV)

2. Armor: The Christian has defenses that are metaphorically called *armor*, which protect him or her from Satan's devices.

    CENTRAL PASSAGE:

    Therefore take up the whole armor of God, that you may be able to withstand in the evil day, and having done all, to stand. (Ephesians 6:13 NKJV)

3. Resistance: Once the Christian is aware of Satan's intentions and is using the "spiritual armor" discussed in Ephesians 6, he or she may resist any suspected Satanic advances with confidence of victory.

    CENTRAL PASSAGE:

    Therefore submit to God. Resist the devil and he will flee from you. (James 4:7 NKJV)

SELF-TEST

A. The believer's defenses are:

1. A *witness*
2. A *mor*
3. R *esistence*

TEN GREAT DOCTRINES OF THE BIBLE

(From memory, fill in the names of doctrines one through five. See the Appendix for answers.)

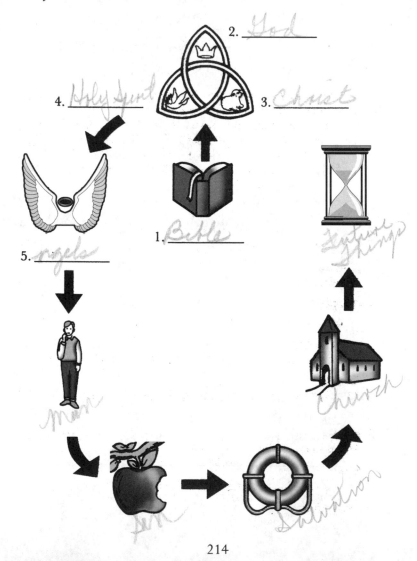

2. *God*

4. *Holy Spirit*   3. *Christ*

1. *Bible*

Future things

5. *ngels*

Church

man

sin   *Salvation*

CHAPTER TWENTY-SIX

THE DOCTRINE OF MAN

IN THIS CHAPTER, WE USE THE WORD "MAN" IN ITS CLASSICAL and biblical sense, as synonymous with "humanity" or "mankind." As we see in Genesis 1:27, this term includes both male and female.

If the full power of the human mind were manifested by an individual, the world would assume that person was a god. The power of the brain is beyond comprehension. Scientists estimate that the most brilliant among us use perhaps 10 percent of its capacity. Yet that might be wildly overstated when we ponder glimpses of its potential.

Mozart wrote his first full-length orchestral piece when he was only eight years old. Amazing as that is, it pales in comparison with other possibilities.

One of the most arresting speculations arises from an observation of people suffering from the "idiot-savant" syndrome. These people are individuals who for the most part are severely retarded. Yet they sometimes possess astounding powers in very limited areas.

There are twins from New York who can calculate the day of the week of any date you mention. If asked in which months and years of this century the twenty-first will fall on a Thursday, the brothers can give you the correct answer instantly.

Another savant can hear a long, intricate classical piano piece for the first time and immediately sit down at a piano without the music and play it back flawlessly.

Another man from Edinburgh, Scotland, is legally blind and so severely retarded he can barely speak. Yet he draws pictures with crayons that betray the skill of a master and are sold for exorbitant prices around the world.

The minds of savants are like calculators or tape recorders or cameras—able to capture the specific details of pictures or songs or mathematical formulas and then use those details with exacting precision.

Perhaps these examples give us a glimpse of what God originally intended our whole mind to be capable of doing.

The indications from Scripture suggest that man's capacity before the Fall and his capacity once restored and glorified in heaven are unimaginable. Someone once wrote that if we were to see our glorified selves walking down the street toward us, we would be tempted to fall at our feet and worship ourselves. Such is the future of humanity in Christ.

I. Review: Fill in the blanks.

THE DOCTRINE OF THE BIBLE

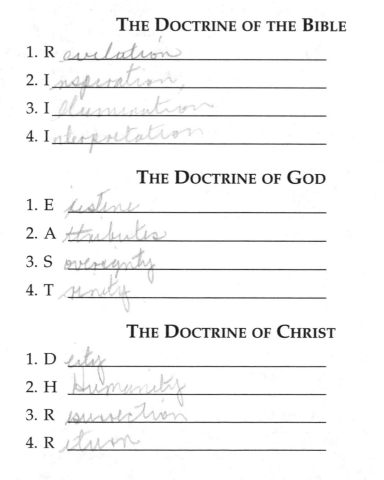

1. R _revelation_
2. I _nspiration_
3. I _llumination_
4. I _nterpretation_

THE DOCTRINE OF GOD

1. E _xistence_
2. A _ttributes_
3. S _overeignty_
4. T _rinity_

THE DOCTRINE OF CHRIST

1. D _eity_
2. H _umanity_
3. R _esurrection_
4. R _eturn_

THE DOCTRINE OF THE HOLY SPIRIT

1. P _ersonality_
2. D _eity_
3. S _alvation_
4. G _ifts_

THE DOCTRINE OF ANGELS

1. A _ngels_
2. D _emons_
3. S _atan_
4. D _efenses_

II. The Four Major Subdivisions of the Doctrine of Man Are:

1. Origin

2. Nature

3. Distinctiveness

4. Destiny

(As you read the definitions of the doctrine subdivisions, notice the words in italics. Immediately following the definitions, they are repeated with blank spaces in place of the italic words. Fill in the blank spaces.)

SYMBOL: **SUBDIVISION:**   **DEFINITION:**

1. Origin: Man was *created* by God in His image.

   Origin: Man was ___*created*___ by God in His image.

Man's purpose is to "know God and enjoy Him forever." Man was *created* in perfect fellowship and harmony with God, in His image. This does not mean physical likeness, for God does not have a physical body. But it means in the psychological, emotional, and spiritual likeness of God.

CENTRAL PASSAGE:

And God created man in His own image, in the image of God He created him; male and female He created them. (Genesis 1:27)

SYMBOL: **SUBDIVISION:**   **DEFINITION:**

2. Nature: Man has a *spiritual* as well as a physical dimension.

   Nature: Man has a ___*spiritual*___ as well as a physical dimension.

Man is *spiritual* as well as physical. Man's earthly physical body is destined to die. The moment he is born, the process is set in motion for him to die. His spirit, however, lives forever and transcends his physical limitations. After man dies, he receives a new body that lives forever.

CENTRAL PASSAGE:

Now may the God of peace Himself sanctify you entirely; and may your spirit and soul and body be preserved complete, without blame at the coming of our Lord Jesus Christ. (1 Thessalonians 5:23)

SYMBOL: **SUBDIVISION:**   **DEFINITION:**

3. Distinctiveness: Man has *capacities* that go beyond those of any animals and mark him as the pinnacle of God's creation.

Distinctiveness: Man has *capacities* that go beyond those of any animals and mark him as the pinnacle of God's creation.

Man possesses intellect, emotion, and will. With intellect he can know, reason, and think. With emotion he can feel, empathize, and experience. With will he can choose. These are all characteristics of God and, as such, are part of the "image of God" within man. In addition, man has the capacity for self-awareness, an awareness of God, an awareness of afterlife, and the ability to envision life in the future under different scenarios such as heaven and hell, etc. Man certainly has characteristics that overlap with the animals, but his capacities not only go beyond those of animals, he has *capacities* that no animals have.

CENTRAL PASSAGE:

Then God said, "Let Us make man in Our image, according to Our likeness; and let them rule over the fish of the sea and over the birds of the sky and over the cattle and over all the earth, and over every creeping thing that creeps on the earth." (Genesis 1:26)

SYMBOL:	SUBDIVISION:	DEFINITION:

4. Destiny: Man will live *forever* in heaven or hell.

Destiny: Man will live *forever* in heaven or hell.

Though man's spirit inhabits a body at all times, that body changes after death on earth. A new body is received, depending on his destiny, in which he will continue to live *forever.*

Destiny in hell is portrayed as agonizing torment, though little is known of the specifics of that torment. Existence in heaven is pictured in great detail, though we still might wish for more details. The heavenly body is beautiful beyond imagination, exceedingly powerful, and not subject to time and space limitations. The citizen of heaven will rule in the celestial realm and will possess power, wisdom, and unbounded creativity. Greater attention will be given to man's destiny later in this chapter and in the chapter on the doctrine of future things.

CENTRAL PASSAGE:

It is appointed for men to die once and after this comes judgment. (Hebrews 9:27)

The Doctrine of Man

(Write the titles of the four subdivisions on the lines below.)

SYMBOL:	SUBDIVISION:	DEFINITION:

1. Origin — Man was *created* by God in His image.

CENTRAL PASSAGE: Genesis 1:27

SYMBOL:

SUBDIVISION:

2. Nature

DEFINITION:

Man has a *spiritual* as well as a physical dimension.

CENTRAL PASSAGE: 1 Thessalonians 5:23

SYMBOL:

SUBDIVISION:

3. Distinctiveness

DEFINITION:

Man has *capacities* that go beyond those of any animals and mark him as the pinnacle of God's creation.

CENTRAL PASSAGE: Genesis 1:26

SYMBOL:

SUBDIVISION:

4. Destiny

DEFINITION:

Man will live *forever* in heaven or hell.

CENTRAL PASSAGE: Hebrews 9:27

THE DOCTRINE OF MAN

(Name the four subdivisions of the doctrine of man and fill in the key words in the definitions.)

SYMBOL:

SUBDIVISION:

1. Origin

DEFINITION:

Man was created by God in His image.

CENTRAL PASSAGE: Genesis 1:27

SYMBOL:

SUBDIVISION:

2. Nature

DEFINITION:

Man has a spiritual as well as a physical dimension.

CENTRAL PASSAGE: 1 Thessalonians 5:23

SYMBOL:

SUBDIVISION:

3. Distinctiveness

DEFINITION:

Man has capacities that go beyond those of any animals and mark him as the pinnacle of God's creation.

CENTRAL PASSAGE: Genesis 1:26

SYMBOL: SUBDIVISION: DEFINITION:

4. *Destiny*   Man will live *forever* in heaven or hell.

CENTRAL PASSAGE: Hebrews 9:27

SELF-TEST

(Fill in the blanks.)

1. O*rigin*   Man was *created* by God in His image.

2. N*ature*   Man has a *spiritual* as well as a physical dimension.

3. D*istinctiveness* Man has *capacities* that go beyond those of any animals and mark him as the pinnacle of God's creation.

4. D*estiny*   Man will live *forever* in heaven or hell.

TEN GREAT DOCTRINES OF THE BIBLE

(From memory, fill in the names of doctrines one through six. See the Appendix for answers.)

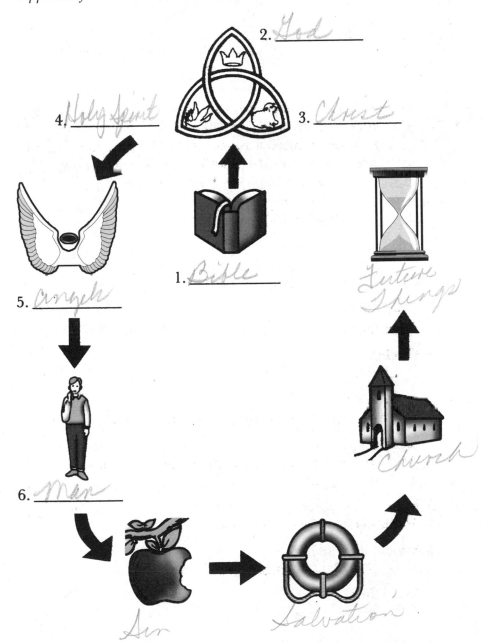

2. *God*

4. *Holy Spirit*

3. *Christ*

1. *Bible*

5. *angels*

Future Things

6. *Man*

Church

Sin

Salvation

CHAPTER TWENTY-SEVEN

THE DOCTRINE OF SIN

 I GREW UP IN RURAL NORTHERN INDIANA WHERE PIG FARMING is common. I used to have to work among the pigs, feeding them, tending to their physical and medical needs, and cleaning up after them. If you have never worked around farm animals, you probably cannot imagine how bad a pen in a barn stinks when pigs have been shut up in it all winter. It will bring tears to your eyes, take your breath away, and cause you to long for a white-collar job.

But one thing I noticed. The pigs didn't mind it. I never saw a pig walk into a pen, sniff the air in disgust, and turn around and walk out because the place smelled so bad. It always seemed OK to the pig. Every pig I ever saw looked completely at home in a pigpen.

When it comes to sin, we're a little like the pigs. The smell of sin doesn't seem so bad to us. We don't even notice a lot of it. But to God, it smells like a thousand pigs that were kept in His living room for the winter.

Man does not and cannot grasp the awfulness of sin to the degree God does. But for two reasons we must try to grasp as much as we can. First, sin is harmful to us; it is self-destructive. All sins are boomerangs; they come back to hurt us every time. Second, sin grieves God, and if we hope to live a life pleasing to Him, we must try to live a life of righteousness.

I. **Review:** Fill in the blanks.

THE DOCTRINE OF THE BIBLE

1. R_evelation_
2. I_nspiration_
3. I_llumination_
4. I_nterpretation_

THE DOCTRINE OF GOD

1. E *xistence*
2. A *ttributes*
3. S *overeignty*
4. T *rinity*

THE DOCTRINE OF CHRIST

1. D *eity*
2. H *umanity*
3. R *esurrection*
4. R *eturn*

THE DOCTRINE OF THE HOLY SPIRIT

1. P *ersonality*
2. D *eity*
3. S *alvation*
4. G *ifts*

THE DOCTRINE OF ANGELS

1. A *ngels*
2. D *emons*
3. S *atan*
4. D *efense*

THE DOCTRINE OF MAN

1. O *rigin*
2. N *ature*
3. D *istinctiveness*
4. D *estiny*

II. The Four Major Subdivisions of the Doctrine of Sin Are:

 1. Nature

 2. Fall

 3. Corruption

 4. Rebellion

(As you read the definitions of the doctrine subdivisions, notice the words in italics. Immediately following the definitions, they are repeated with blank spaces in place of the italic words. Fill in the blank spaces.)

SYMBOL:	SUBDIVISION:	DEFINITION:
	1. Nature:	Sin is any lack of conformity to the moral *perfection* of God.
	Nature:	Sin is any lack of conformity to the moral ___perfection___ of God.

All that is good, right, and pleasant comes from God. Anything that does not come from God is the opposite. By definition, it must be bad, wrong, and unpleasant. We are creatures who sin. When we do, we bring bad, wrong, and unpleasant things into our lives, we diminish the reputation of God as His children, and we decrease the interest the non-

Christian world might have in God because they do not see the difference between being Christian and not being Christian.

CENTRAL PASSAGE:

All unrighteousness is sin. (1 John 5:17)

SYMBOL:	SUBDIVISION:	DEFINITION:
	2. Fall:	The *separation* of Adam and Eve from God in the Garden of Eden because of original sin.
	Fall:	The _separation_ of Adam and Eve from God in the Garden of Eden because of original sin.

All the pain, all the evil, all the suffering that is in the world, that has ever been in the world, and that will ever be in the world can be traced back to one event: when Adam and Eve disobeyed God in the Garden. Because of the cataclysmically negative effects of that event, it has been referred to as the Fall of man.

CENTRAL PASSAGE:

When the woman saw that the tree was good for food, and that it was a delight to the eyes, and that the tree was desirable to make one wise, she took from its fruit and ate; and she gave also to her husband with her, and he ate. (Genesis 3:6)

SYMBOL:	SUBDIVISION:	DEFINITION:
	3. Corruption:	Mankind as a whole was *corrupted* by the original Fall.
	Corruption:	Mankind as a whole was _corrupted_ by the original Fall.

Sin entered mankind, and now all men are corrupted with sin. It is not that man is not capable of doing good (for certainly some people do wonderful things), or even that he is as bad as he could be (many people could be much worse than they are). It is just that he cannot keep from doing that which is bad, because his essential nature has been corrupted. David said, "in sin my mother conceived me" (Psalm 51:5). This does not mean that his mother sinned, but that all men are born sinners. We are not sinners because we sin. We sin because we are sinners.

CENTRAL PASSAGE:

And you were dead in your trespasses and sins. . . . Among them we too all formerly lived in the lusts of our flesh, indulging the desires of the flesh and of the mind, and were by nature children of wrath. (Ephesians 2:1, 3)

SYMBOL:	SUBDIVISION:	DEFINITION:
	4. Rebellion:	Because man's internal nature has been corrupted by sin, he cannot keep from committing *personal* sins.
	Rebellion:	Because man's internal nature has been corrupted by sin, he cannot keep from committing _personal_ sins.

Man's heart has been corrupted, and therefore he commits individual, personal sins. Some of these sins are sins of commission (things we ought not to do, but do) and some are sins of omission (things we ought to do but don't). They may be tangible acts, or they may be deficient attitudes, motives, or perspectives. When we compare ourselves with

228

other people on external things, we might not do so badly. But when we compare ourselves with Jesus, who had no imperfections in act, thought, motive, word, or deed, we see that we fall short.

CENTRAL PASSAGES:

For all have sinned and fall short of the glory of God. . . . For the wages of sin is death. (Romans 3:23 and 6:23)

THE DOCTRINE OF SIN

(Write the titles of the four subdivisions on the lines below.)

SYMBOL:	SUBDIVISION:	DEFINITION:
	1. N_ature_	Sin is any lack of conformity to the moral *perfection* of God.

CENTRAL PASSAGE: 1 John 5:17

SYMBOL:	SUBDIVISION:	DEFINITION:
	2. F_all_	The *separation* of Adam and Eve from God in the Garden of Eden because of original sin.

CENTRAL PASSAGE: Genesis 3:6

SYMBOL:	SUBDIVISION:	DEFINITION:
	3. C_orruption_	Mankind as a whole was *corrupted* by the original Fall.

CENTRAL PASSAGE: Ephesians 2:1, 3

SYMBOL:	SUBDIVISION:	DEFINITION:
	4. R_ebellion_	Because man's internal nature has been corrupted by sin, he cannot keep from committing *personal* sins.

CENTRAL PASSAGES: Romans 3:23 and 6:23

THE DOCTRINE OF SIN

(Name the four subdivisions of the doctrine of sin and fill in the key words in the definitions.)

SYMBOL: **SUBDIVISION:**   **DEFINITION:**

1. *Nature*   Sin is any lack of conformity to the moral *perfection* of God.

CENTRAL PASSAGE: 1 John 5:17

SYMBOL: **SUBDIVISION:**   **DEFINITION:**

2. *Fall*   The *separation* of Adam and Eve from God in the Garden of Eden because of original sin.

CENTRAL PASSAGE: Genesis 3:6

SYMBOL: **SUBDIVISION:**   **DEFINITION:**

3. *Corruption*   Mankind as a whole was *corrupted* by the original Fall.

CENTRAL PASSAGE: Ephesians 2:1, 3

SYMBOL: **SUBDIVISION:**   **DEFINITION:**

4. *Rebellion*   Because man's internal nature has been corrupted by sin, he cannot keep from committing *personal* sins.

CENTRAL PASSAGES: Romans 3:23 and 6:23

SELF-TEST

(Fill in the blanks.)

1. N*ature*   Sin is any lack of conformity to the moral *perfection* of God.

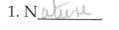

2. F_*all*___ The _separation_ of Adam and Eve from God in the Garden of Eden because of original sin.

3. C*orruption* Mankind as a whole was _corrupted_ by the original Fall.

4. R*ebellion* Because man's internal nature has been corrupted by sin, he cannot keep from committing _personal_ sins.

TEN GREAT DOCTRINES OF THE BIBLE

(From memory, fill in the names of doctrines one through seven. See the Appendix for answers.)

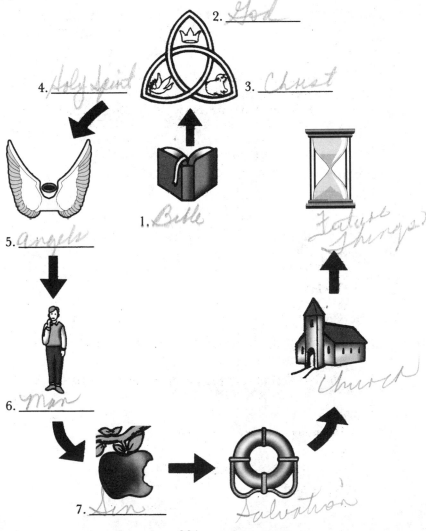

2. _God_

4. _Holy Spirit_

3. _Christ_

1. _Bible_

5. _angels_

6. _Man_

7. _Sin_

Future Things

Church

Salvation

231

CHAPTER TWENTY-EIGHT

THE DOCTRINE OF SALVATION

 IN STUDYING THE MATTER OF MAN'S DESTINY, WE ACTUALLY overlap with our overview of the Doctrine of Salvation. We saw earlier that man has a spirit as well as a body and that he will live forever in heaven or hell. The immediate concern, then, is what determines his destiny? The Bible appears to teach that children who die before the age of accountability, that is, the age at which they have the intellectual capacity to accept or reject God, go to heaven. After they reach that age, if they do not accept God's salvation before they die, they will go to hell. How, then, does man avoid that destiny? What is the basis of God's salvation?

There are several commonly held beliefs about how to get to heaven. One belief suggests that if no really terrible sins are committed, God will overlook the small ones. Another suggests that if your good works outweigh your bad works at the end of your life, you will make it to heaven. Still another suggests that God will line up all the people in the world who ever lived, from the worst to the best, and divide that line in half. The worst go to hell, and the best go to heaven. All these beliefs are incorrect. Good and bad works have absolutely nothing to do with whether or not you go to heaven.

I. **Review:** Fill in the blanks.

THE DOCTRINE OF THE BIBLE

1. R *evelation*
2. I *nspiration*
3. I *illumination*
4. I *nterpretation*

THE DOCTRINE OF GOD

1. E _xistence_
2. A _ttributes_
3. S _overeignty_
4. T _rinity_

THE DOCTRINE OF CHRIST

1. D _eity_
2. H _umanity_
3. R _esurrection_
4. R _eturn_

THE DOCTRINE OF THE HOLY SPIRIT

1. P _ersonality_
2. D _eity_
3. S _alvation_
4. G _ifts_

THE DOCTRINE OF ANGELS

1. A _ngels_
2. D _emons_
3. S _atan_
4. D _efeness_

THE DOCTRINE OF MAN

1. O _rigin_
2. N _ature_
3. D _istinctiveness_
4. D _estiny_

THE DOCTRINE OF SIN

1. N *ature*

2. F *all*

3. C *orruption*

4. R *ebellion*

II. The Four Major Subdivisions of the Doctrine of Salvation Are:

1. Basis

2. Result

3. Cost

4. Timing

(As you read the definitions of the doctrine subdivisions, notice the words in italics. Immediately following the definitions, they are repeated with blank spaces in place of the italic words. Fill in the blank spaces.)

SYMBOL:	SUBDIVISION:	DEFINITION:

1. Basis: Salvation is a *gift* God gives to those who believe.

Basis: Salvation is a ___*gift*___ God gives to those who believe.

We cannot earn our salvation. We are imperfect, and we cannot make ourselves perfect. Yet God demands perfection. Therefore, all we can do is cast ourselves on God's mercy. In His mercy, God offers to forgive our sin and *give* us a new nature of holiness so that we can be in perfect relationship with Him. The completion of that relationship is not realized until we die and we shed the "body of sin" in which we live. God's offer has one condition: that we believe in and receive Jesus as our Savior.

CENTRAL PASSAGE:

For by grace you have been saved through faith; and that not of yourselves, it is the gift of God; not as a result of works, that no one should boast. (Ephesians 2:8, 9)

SYMBOL:	SUBDIVISION:	DEFINITION:

2. Result: God extends *forgiveness* of sin and eternal life to those who accept Him.

Result: God extends ___*forgiveness*___ of sin and eternal life to those who accept Him.

God's solution to man's inherent dilemma is to offer him *forgiveness* of his sins and to give him a new nature that is not flawed. Man still languishes under the impact of sin until his flawed body dies and he receives a new body. Then he is free to serve God forever in heaven in undiluted righteousness.

CENTRAL PASSAGE:

Therefore having been justified by faith, we have peace with God through our Lord Jesus Christ. (Romans 5:1)

SYMBOL:	SUBDIVISION:	DEFINITION:

3. Cost: The penalty of sin is paid for by the *substitutionary* death of Christ.

Cost: The penalty of sin is paid for by the _substitutionary_ death of Christ.

Sin brings death. Since all have sinned, all have died, spiritually, and are separated from God. Jesus was without sin, and He willingly died with the understanding that His death could count as a *substitution* for our own. If you believe in Jesus and receive Him as your personal Savior, God will then count His death for yours and give you eternal life.

CENTRAL PASSAGE:

For Christ also died for sins once for all, the just for the unjust, in order that He might bring us to God, having been put to death in the flesh, but made alive in the spirit. (1 Peter 3:18)

SYMBOL:	SUBDIVISION:	DEFINITION:

4. Timing: Our salvation is completed at the *death* of the *body*.

Timing: Our salvation is completed at the _death_ of the _body_.

Man is body and spirit. Upon becoming a Christian, a person's spirit is born again and he is given eternal life. His body, at that point, remains unchanged. It is corrupted by sin, is susceptible to disease and death, and is inclined to sin. The brain, which is part of the physical body, is still encumbered with old programming that is counter to biblical truth. Because of this, the Christian experiences a continuous struggle between the new inner man who wishes to serve God and the outer man who feels the pull to sin (see Romans 7). This conflict continues until the *death* of the *body*, at which time the spirit of the Christian is transported immediately to heaven to receive a new body, untouched by sin. (Romans 8.23)

Fortunately, until our salvation is completed with "the redemption of the body," when we sin after having become a Christian, "we have an advocate with the Father, Jesus Christ the righteous" (1 John 2:1). "If we confess our sins, He is faithful and righteous to forgive us our sins and to cleanse us from all unrighteousness" (1 John 1:9). God does not want us to sin, but He recognizes that as long as we are in this body, we will. When we do, He cleanses us. The death of Christ on the Cross was sufficient for all our sins, past and future. God is continuously working in our lives, however, to lead us to a more righteous lifestyle. If we resist this work of God, He chastens us, as any loving father would a child, to correct inappropriate behavior. (See Hebrews 12:4–13.)

CENTRAL PASSAGE:

And not only this, but also we ourselves, having the first fruits of the Spirit, even we ourselves groan within ourselves, waiting eagerly for our adoption as sons, the redemption of our body. (Romans 8:23)

THE DOCTRINE OF SALVATION

(Write the titles of the four subdivisions on the lines below.)

SYMBOL: **SUBDIVISION:**   **DEFINITION:**

1. B*asis*   Salvation is a *gift* God gives to those who believe.

CENTRAL PASSAGE: Ephesians 2:8, 9

SYMBOL: **SUBDIVISION:**   **DEFINITION:**

2. R*esult*   God extends *forgiveness* of sin and eternal life to those who accept Him.

CENTRAL PASSAGE: Romans 5:1

SYMBOL: **SUBDIVISION:**   **DEFINITION:**

3. C*ost*   The penalty of sin is paid for by the *substitutionary* death of Christ.

CENTRAL PASSAGE: 1 Peter 3:18

SYMBOL: **SUBDIVISION:**   **DEFINITION:**

4. T*iming*   Our salvation is completed at the *death* of the *body.*

CENTRAL PASSAGE: Romans 8:23

THE DOCTRINE OF SALVATION

(Name the four subdivisions of the doctrine of salvation and fill in the key words in the definition.)

SYMBOL: **SUBDIVISION:**   **DEFINITION:**

1. *Basis*   Salvation is a *gift* God gives to those who believe.

CENTRAL PASSAGE: Ephesians 2:8, 9

SYMBOL:	SUBDIVISION:	DEFINITION:
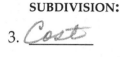	2. *Result*	God extends *forgiveness* of sin and eternal *life* to those who accept Him.

CENTRAL PASSAGE: Romans 5:1

SYMBOL:	SUBDIVISION:	DEFINITION:
	3. *Cost*	The penalty of sin is paid for by the *substitutionary* death of Christ.

CENTRAL PASSAGE: 1 Peter 3:18

SYMBOL:	SUBDIVISION:	DEFINITION:
	4. *Timing*	Our salvation is completed at the *death* of the *body*.

CENTRAL PASSAGE: Romans 8:23

SELF-TEST

(Fill in the blanks.)

1. B*asis*   Salvation is a *gift*   God gives to those who believe.

2. R*esult*   God extends *forgiveness* of sin and eternal life to those who accept Him.

3. C*ost*   The penalty of sin is paid for by the *substitutionary* death of Christ.

4. T*iming*   Our salvation is completed at the *death* of the *body* .

TEN GREAT DOCTRINES OF THE BIBLE

(From memory, fill in the names of doctrines one through eight. See the Appendix for answers.)

2. God

4. Holy Spirit

3. Christ

1. Bible

5. angels

Future Things

6. Man

Churches

7. Sin

8. Salvation

CHAPTER TWENTY-NINE

THE DOCTRINE OF THE CHURCH

THE CHURCH IS TO BE THE PHYSICAL REPRESENTATION OF Christ on earth now that He has returned to heaven. What Christ said, we are to say. What Christ did, we are to do. The message Christ proclaimed, we are to proclaim, and the character Christ manifested, we are to manifest. The world can no longer see Christ living on earth. He is removed physically, though He lives in the hearts of His children. Because the world can no longer see Christ living on earth, it should be able to get a pretty good idea of Christ by looking at His church.

The church is a wonderfully important institution that has fallen into some disregard in the United States lately, even among Christians. It happened partially because many in the mainline denominations abandoned the historic fundamentals of the faith for a form of Christianity that denied the very things that were distinctive to Christianity. When that happened, the church lost its justification for its existence, and attendance began to drop precipitously.

Then a remnant church exerted itself; it was made up largely of newer denominations and independent churches, as well as some churches and denominations that had held firm or renewed themselves. The renewed churches disdained the theological shallowness of churches that had denied their faith and, as a result, they "threw the baby out with the bath water." Out with the theological shallowness went deep respect for tradition, church authority, and the clergy.

But, as Augustine said, "He cannot have God for his father who does not have the church for his mother." The time has come for a resurgence of respect for the church, the Great Bride of Christ, and to hold her with the same regard with which God holds her. The time has come to believe Jesus' promise: "I will build My church." We humbly ask Him, "What would you have me to do?"

I. **Review:** Fill in the blanks.

THE DOCTRINE OF THE BIBLE

1. R *evelation*
2. I *nspiration*
3. I *llumination*
4. I *nterpretation*

THE DOCTRINE OF GOD

1. E *xistence*
2. A *ttributes*
3. S *overeignty*
4. T *rinity*

THE DOCTRINE OF CHRIST

1. D *eity*
2. H *umanity*
3. R *esurrection*
4. R *eturn*

THE DOCTRINE OF THE HOLY SPIRIT

1. P *ersonality*
2. D *eity*
3. S *alvation*
4. G *ifts*

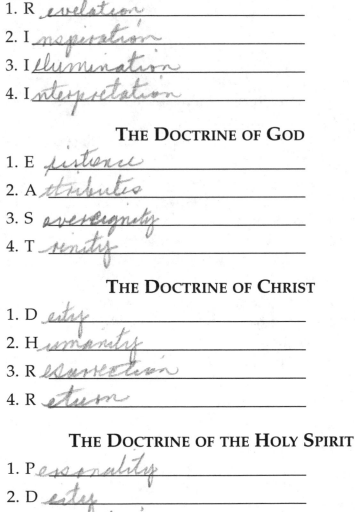

THE DOCTRINE OF ANGELS

1. A *ngels*
2. D *emons*
3. S *atan*
4. D *efenses*

THE DOCTRINE OF MAN

1. O *rigin*
2. N *ature*
3. D *istinctiveness*
4. D *estiny*

THE DOCTRINE OF SIN

1. N *ature*
2. F *all*
3. C *orruption*
4. R *ebellion*

THE DOCTRINE OF SALVATION

1. B *Basis*
2. R *Result*
3. C *ost*
4. R *Timing*

II. **The Four Major Subdivisions of the Doctrine of the Church Are:**

    1. Universal Church

2. Local Church

 3. Leadership

 4. Membership

(As you read the definitions of the doctrine subdivisions, notice the words in italics. Immediately following the definitions, they are repeated with blank spaces in place of the italic words. Fill in the blank spaces.)

SYMBOL:	SUBDIVISION:	DEFINITION:
	1. Universal	The universal church is the church: totality of all *believers* in Jesus.
	Universal	The universal church is the church: totality of all _believers_ in Jesus.

The universal church, also called the body of Christ (Colossians 1:24), refers to all people in all parts of the world who have become Christians since the beginning of the church and who will become Christians before Christ returns. The church began on the day of Pentecost (Acts 2), and will culminate when Christ returns. Christ is the head of the church (Colossians 1:18), and the universal church is to be the representation of Christ on earth, collectively doing His will.

CENTRAL PASSAGE:

And I say to you that you are Peter, and on this rock I will build my church, and the gates of Hades shall not prevail against it. (Matthew 16:18)

SYMBOL:	SUBDIVISION:	DEFINITION:

2. Local Church: A local assembly of believers *organized* to carry out the responsibilities of the universal church.

Local Church: A local assembly of believers ~~organized~~ to carry out the responsibilities of the universal church.

The church is not a building, but people. At any given time and place, Christians are to band together to carry out the responsibilities of the universal church. As such, they organize to govern themselves, select spiritual leaders, collect money for ministry, observe baptism and communion, exercise church discipline, engage in mutual edification and evangelism, and worship God.

CENTRAL PASSAGE:

Paul, called as an apostle of Jesus Christ by the will of God, . . . to the church of God which is at Corinth. (1 Corinthians 1:1, 2)

SYMBOL:	SUBDIVISION:	DEFINITION:

3. Leadership: Those in the church worthy of being followed because of their *spiritual* maturity.

Leadership: Those in the church worthy of being followed because of their ~~spiritual~~ maturity.

Leadership in the local church is invested in pastor-teachers, elders, and deacons and deaconesses. The Scripture appears to give freedom as to how this leadership is organized and functions, but it is quite specific about the spiritual qualifications. Only spiritually mature people are to be given high positions of spiritual leadership in the church.

CENTRAL PASSAGE:

An overseer, then, must be above reproach, the husband of one wife, temperate, prudent, respectable, hospitable, able to teach, not addicted to wine or pugnacious, but gentle, uncontentious, free from the love of money. He must be one who manages his own household well, keeping his children under control with all dignity . . . and not a new convert, . . . and he must have a good reputation with those outside the church. (1 Timothy 3:2–4, 6, 7)

SYMBOL:	SUBDIVISION:	DEFINITION:

4. Membership: *Belonging* to the universal church and a local church.

Membership: <u>Belonging</u> to the universal church and a local church.

When a person becomes a Christian, he or she immediately and automatically becomes a member of the universal church, the body of Christ. Throughout church history, local churches have had varying requirements for membership that range from very limited to very strict. This appears to be a point of freedom given local churches in the Scripture. An important point, however, is that everyone should be a part of a local church. God never intended for Christians to try to make it alone. Placing oneself under spiritual authority and in mutual ministry with others is essential to spiritual health.

CENTRAL PASSAGE:

Let us consider how to stimulate one another to love and good deeds, not forsaking our own assembling together, as is the habit of some, but encouraging one another; and all the more, as you see the day drawing near. (Hebrews 10:24, 25)

THE DOCTRINE OF THE CHURCH

(Write the titles of the four subdivisions on the lines below.)

SYMBOL:	SUBDIVISION:	DEFINITION:

1. U*niversal Church*

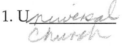

The universal church is the totality of all *believers* in Jesus.

CENTRAL PASSAGE: Ephesians 5:25, 27

SYMBOL:	SUBDIVISION:	DEFINITION:

2. L*ocal Church*

A local assembly of believers *organized* to carry out the responsibilities of the universal church.

CENTRAL PASSAGE: 1 Corinthians 1:1, 2

SYMBOL:	SUBDIVISION:	DEFINITION:

3. L*eadership*

Those in the church worthy of being followed because of their *spiritual* maturity.

CENTRAL PASSAGE: 1 Timothy 3:2–4, 6, 7

SYMBOL:	SUBDIVISION:	DEFINITION:

4. M*embership*

Belonging to the universal church and a local church.

CENTRAL PASSAGE: Hebrews 10:24, 25

THE DOCTRINE OF THE CHURCH

(Name the four subdivisions of the doctrine of the church and fill in the key words in the definitions.)

SYMBOL:

SUBDIVISION:

1. *Universal*

DEFINITION:

The universal church is the totality of all *believers* in Jesus.

CENTRAL PASSAGE: Ephesians 5:25, 27

SYMBOL:

SUBDIVISION:

2. *Local Church*

DEFINITION:

A local assembly of believers *organized* to carry out the responsibilities of the universal church.

CENTRAL PASSAGE: 1 Corinthians 1:1, 2

SYMBOL:

SUBDIVISION:

3. *Leadership*

DEFINITION:

Those in the church worthy of being followed because of their *spiritual* maturity.

CENTRAL PASSAGE: 1 Timothy 3:2–4, 6, 7

SYMBOL:

SUBDIVISION:

4. *Membership*

DEFINITION:

Belonging to the universal church and a local church.

CENTRAL PASSAGE: Hebrews 10:24, 25

SELF-TEST

(Fill in the blanks.)

1. U*niversal Church* — The universal church is the totality of all *believers* in Jesus.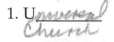

2. L*ocal Church* — A local assembly of believers *organized* to carry out the responsibilities of the universal church.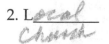

3. L_*Leadership*_ Those in the church worthy of being followed because of their _*spiritual*_ maturity.

4. M_*embership*_ _*Belonging*_ to the universal church and a local church.

TEN GREAT DOCTRINES OF THE BIBLE

(From memory, fill in the names of doctrines one through nine. See the Appendix for answers.)

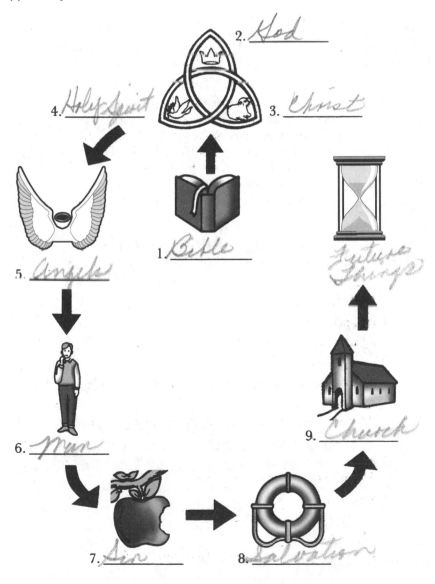

2. *God*

4. *Holy Spirit*

3. *Christ*

1. *Bible*

5. *Angels*

6. *Man*

9. *Church*

Future Things

7. *Sin*

8. *Salvation*

CHAPTER THIRTY

THE DOCTRINE OF FUTURE THINGS

THE STORY OF LITTLE LORD FAUNTLEROY IS AN ENGAGING and instructive one. The son of an English earl marries an American woman and is consequently disinherited. Some years later, he dies at sea and his widow and son live humbly in New York City. The disinherited man's father, the Earl of Darringcourt, becomes aged and is concerned for the succession to his fortune and family line. His ten-year-old American grandson is his only legal heir, so he sends a representative to America to offer to have his grandson come to live on the fabulous estate as Lord Fauntleroy and eventually succeed him as Earl of Darringcourt. There is one catch. Little Lord Fauntleroy's American mother, who was the cause of the original disinheritance, an exemplary woman with whom Lord Fauntleroy is very close, cannot live on the estate. The story of the initial conflict and misunderstanding and the subsequent healing and restoration of relationships is a touching one in which everyone eventually lives happily ever after.

When the Earl of Darringcourt's representative first comes to America with the proposal, a circumstance arises that is analogous to the life of a Christian. He describes what life will be like as Lord Fauntleroy. Wealth, power, honor, and glory are his. He is a royal heir. Yet he will have to wait until he gets to England to experience it. For now, he will have some limited benefits, but for the most part, until he crosses the Atlantic, the life of Lord Fauntleroy has to wait.

The situation for the Christian is similar. The Bible presents a picture of a future that is difficult to imagine. Power, glory, wealth, and honor are ours. But in large measure, we must wait until we get to heaven to experience it. For now, the limitations of earth are very much with us. Until we cross the Atlantic, the life of Lord Fauntleroy will have to wait.

The information the Bible presents about Future Things is sketchy. The prophetic information in the Bible is not given to satisfy our innate curiosity about the future, but to encourage us to live like royalty while we are still here on earth. It is given, not to impact our curiosity, but our lifestyle.

Therefore, while the information is incomplete as to details we might desire to know, it is adequate for us to take our present life seriously. We are royalty with a celestial inheritance, but we are presently misplaced.

I. **Review:** Fill in the blanks.

THE DOCTRINE OF THE BIBLE

1. R _evelation_
2. I _nspiration_
3. I _llumination_
4. I _nterpretation_

THE DOCTRINE OF GOD

1. E _xistence_
2. A _ttributes_
3. S _overeignty_
4. T _rinity_

THE DOCTRINE OF CHRIST

1. D _eity_
2. H _umanity_
3. R _esurrection_
4. R _estore_

251

THE DOCTRINE OF THE HOLY SPIRIT

1. P _personality_
2. D _eity_
3. S _alvation_
4. G _ifts_

THE DOCTRINE OF ANGELS

1. A _ngels_
2. D _emons_
3. S _atan_
4. D _efenses_

THE DOCTRINE OF MAN

1. O _rigin_
2. N _ature_
3. D _istinctiveness_
4. D _estiny_

THE DOCTRINE OF SIN

1. N _ature_
2. F _all_
3. C _orruption_
4. R _ebellion_

THE DOCTRINE OF SALVATION

1. N _Basis_
2. F _Result_
3. C _ost_
4. R _Timing_

THE DOCTRINE OF THE CHURCH

1. N *Universal*
2. F *Local*
3. C *Leadership*
4. R *Membership*

II. The Four Major Subdivisions of the Doctrine of Future Things Are:

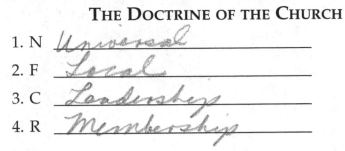

1. Return

2. Judgment

3. Universe

4. Eternity

(As you read the definitions of the doctrine subdivisions, notice the words in italics. Immediately following the definitions, they are repeated with blank spaces in place of the italic words. Fill in the blank spaces.)

SYMBOL:	SUBDIVISION:	DEFINITION:
	1. Return:	Jesus will *return* to earth again.
	Return:	Jesus will *return* to earth again.

Jesus of Nazareth was crucified, buried, and resurrected about A.D. 30. He ascended into heaven, where He has remained for the last two thousand years. At some time in the future, and from prophetic information it could be at any time, He will *return* to earth. When He does, it will not be as a carpenter's son but in power and glory, revealing His true cosmic sovereignty. During His first visit to earth, He came as a servant with an emphasis on His humanity. During His second visit to earth He will come as a King, emphasizing His deity.

CENTRAL PASSAGE:

For the Son of Man is going to come in the glory of His Father with His angels. (Matthew 16:27)

SYMBOL:	SUBDIVISION:	DEFINITION:
	2. Judgment:	God will *confirm* the eternal *destiny* of all individuals.
	Judgment:	God will _Confirm_ the eternal _destiny_ of all individuals.

At two different times and places, God will conduct audiences with all humanity to *confirm* our eternal *destiny.* Those who believed in Jesus and received Him will then be confirmed to eternity in heaven with Him. Those who did not believe in Him and receive Him will be confirmed to eternal separation from Him in hell.

CENTRAL PASSAGE:

For we must all appear before the judgment seat of Christ, that each one may be recompensed for his deeds in the body, according to what he has done, whether good or bad. (2 Corinthians 5:10)

And if anyone's name was not found written in the book of life, he was thrown into the lake of fire. (Revelation 20:15)

SYMBOL:	SUBDIVISION:	DEFINITION:
	3. Universe:	The old universe will be destroyed and *replaced* with a new one.
	Universe:	The old universe will be destroyed and *replaced* with a new one.

The present universe was flawed with sin at the time of the "Fall" of man. While much of nature is beautiful, much of it is also destructive and uninhabitable. The universe will be destroyed with an apocalyptic cosmic fire and *replaced* with a new universe and a new earth that will have no harmful features. (See 2 Peter 3:12, 13 and Revelation 21:4.)

CENTRAL PASSAGE:

And I saw a new heaven and a new earth; for the first heaven and the first earth passed away, and there is no longer any sea. (Revelation 21:1)

SYMBOL:	SUBDIVISION:	DEFINITION:
	4. Eternity:	Christians will live with God *forever.*
	Eternity:	Christians will live with God *forever.*

Jesus will reign in absolute righteousness. Only goodness and beauty will exist. Believers will rule with Him *forever* as vice-regents. They will govern angelic beings. They will be beings of beauty and power who will participate in glorious celestial ceremonies. Believers themselves will receive much personal glory by the grace and goodness of God, as well as spend generous time worshiping and praising God. Intellect, beauty, power, and talent will be virtually limitless as believers both serve Jesus the King and rule with Him in a world that progressively glorifies God and brings great joy and individual satisfaction.

CENTRAL PASSAGE:

In My Father's house are many dwelling places; if it were not so, I would have told you; for I go to prepare a place for you. And if I go and prepare a place for you, I will come again, and receive you to Myself; that where I am, there you may be also. (John 14:2, 3)

And they [Christians] shall reign forever and ever. (Revelation 22:5)

THE DOCTRINE OF FUTURE THINGS

(Write the titles of the four subdivisions on the lines below.)

SYMBOL:

SUBDIVISION:	DEFINITION:
1. R*eturn*	Jesus will *return* to earth again.

CENTRAL PASSAGE: Matthew 16:27

SYMBOL:

SUBDIVISION:	DEFINITION:
2. J*udgment*	God will *confirm* the eternal *destiny* of all individuals.

CENTRAL PASSAGE: 2 Corinthians 5:10; Revelation 20:15

SYMBOL:

SUBDIVISION:	DEFINITION:
3. U*niverse*	The old universe will be destroyed and *replaced* with a new one.

CENTRAL PASSAGE: Revelation 21:1

SYMBOL: **SUBDIVISION:**   **DEFINITION:**

4. E*ternity* 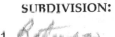   Christians will live with God *forever.*

CENTRAL PASSAGES: John 14:2, 3; Revelation 22:5

THE DOCTRINE OF FUTURE THINGS

(Name the four subdivisions of the doctrine of future things and fill in the key words in the definitions.)

SYMBOL: **SUBDIVISION:**   **DEFINITION:**

1. *Return*   Jesus will *return* to earth again.

CENTRAL PASSAGE: Matthew 16:27

SYMBOL: **SUBDIVISION:**   **DEFINITION:**

2. *Judgment*    God will *confirm* the eternal *destiny* of all individuals.

CENTRAL PASSAGES: 2 Corinthians 5:10; Revelation 20:15

SYMBOL: **SUBDIVISION:**   **DEFINITION:**

3. *Universe*   The old universe will be destroyed and *replaced* with a new one.

CENTRAL PASSAGE: Revelation 21:1

SYMBOL: **SUBDIVISION:**   **DEFINITION:**

4. *Eternity*   Christians will live with God *forever*.

CENTRAL PASSAGES: John 14:2, 3; Revelation 22:5

SELF-TEST

(Fill in the blanks.)

1. R _etern_ Jesus will _return_ to earth again.

2. J_udgment_ God will _confirm_ the eternal _destiny_ of all individuals.

3. U_niverse_ The old universe will be destroyed and _replaced_ with a new one.

4. E_ternity_ Christians will live with God _forever_.

TEN GREAT DOCTRINES OF THE BIBLE

(From memory, fill in the names of all the doctrines. See the Appendix for answers.)

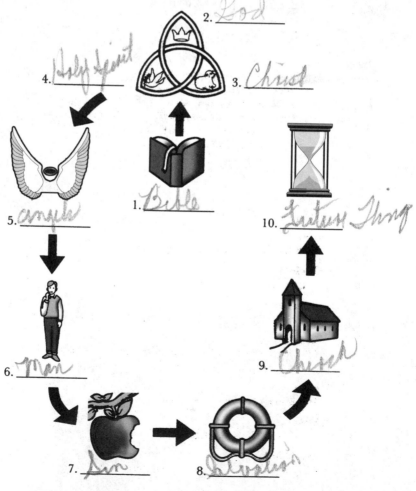

2. _God_

4. _Holy Spirit_

3. _Christ_

1. _Bible_

5. _angels_

10. _Future Things_

6. _Man_

9. _Church_

7. _Sin_

8. _Salvation_

258

Fill in the names of the doctrines and their subdivisions on the lines below:

1. B _ible_ _____
    R _evelation_ _____
    I _nspiration_ _____
    I _llumination_ _____
    I _nterpretation_ _____

2. G _od_ _____
    E _xistence_ _____
    A _ttributes_ _____
    S _overeignty_ _____
    T _rinity_ _____

3. C _hrist_ _____
    D _eity_ _____
    H _umanity_ _____
    R _esurrection_ _____
    R _eturn_ _____

4. H _oly Spirit_ S _____
    P _ersonality_ _____
    D _eity_ _____
    S _alvation_ _____
    G _ifts_ _____

5. A ngels
    A ngels
    D emons
    S atan
    D efenses

6. M an
    O rigin
    N ature
    D istinctiveness
    D estiny

7. S in
    N ature
    F all
    C orruption
    R ebellion

8. S alvation
    B asis
    R esult
    C ost
    T iming

9. C hurch
    U niversal church

L _ocal Church_

L _eadership_

M _embership_

10. F _uture_ T _hings_

R _eturn_

J _udgement_

U _niverse_

E _ternity_

Congratulations! You have just completed an overview of the ten major doctrines of the Bible. There is still much more about Bible doctrines to be learned. In a sense, you have learned a very broad outline, and much of the Bible is dedicated to filling in the outline. Nevertheless, you now have a structure for acquiring an advanced knowledge of the doctrines of the Bible.

CONCLUSION

THE SUMMARY OF THE BIBLE

THE OLD TESTAMENT BEGINS WHEN GOD CREATED ADAM AND EVE IN A perfect paradise. They later sinned and were driven out of the Garden of Eden, forced to live "by the sweat of their brow" in an imperfect world. As their offspring multiplied, sin also multiplied. Eventually, humanity became so sinful that, as judgment, God destroyed the earth with a universal flood, preserving only Noah and his immediate family on the ark to repopulate the earth.

Sin kept its hold over humanity, however, and once again people forgot God. As the years passed, God revealed Himself to Abraham (two thousand years before Christ), promising him a nation, many descendants, and a blessing that would ultimately extend to everyone on the earth. Abraham believed God and became the father of the Hebrew people. Abraham had a son, Isaac, and Isaac had a son, Jacob. The promises God made to Abraham were passed down through Isaac and Jacob. Jacob had twelve sons, and the promises were passed to all twelve sons, who became the fathers of the twelve tribes of Israel.

Jacob and his family of about seventy people were living in the land of Canaan (1) when a famine hit. They were forced to migrate to Egypt (2) to get food. In time, they became so numerous that they were perceived as a threat by the Egyptian people, and the Egyptians enslaved the Hebrew people for nearly four hundred years. Finally (approximately fifteen hundred years before Christ), God raised up Moses to lead them out of Egypt. With many astounding miracles, including the crossing of the Red Sea, they escaped Egypt and went to Mt. Sinai (3), where they received the Ten Commandments. Then they rebelled against God again and, as a judgment, wandered in the wilderness for forty years. When their time of judgment was up, they were allowed to enter the

Promised Land (4). Moses died, and Joshua led in the conquest of the land.

Israel lived in the Promised Land in a loose governmental system ruled by judges for the next four hundred years. Samson and Samuel were the most famous judges. Then Israel insisted on establishing a monarchy (approximately one thousand years before Christ), and the Hebrews were ruled by kings for the next four hundred years. Saul, David, and Solomon were the first three kings, who ruled over a united monarchy for 120 years (forty years each). When Solomon died, the nation divided over the issue of taxation. There was now a northern kingdom, which kept the name Israel, because a majority (ten) of the tribes were loyal to the north, and a southern kingdom, which was called Judah, because Judah was by far the larger of the two southern tribes.

Because of the accumulating sin of Israel, Assyria, a nation to the northeast, came and conquered Israel (5) and scattered many of the people throughout that part of the world (6). About one hundred fifty years later, because of the accumulating sin of Judah, Babylonia came and conquered Judah (7), destroyed Jerusalem, and took many of the people into captivity in Babylonia (8).

About seventy years later, Persia defeated Babylonia, who had previously defeated Assyria. Thus Persia now ruled the entire part of the world from the eastern shores of the Mediterranean Sea to the borders of India. The king of Persia allowed the Israelites living in captivity in Babylonia to return to Jerusalem (9) to rebuild it. Fifty thousand people returned (approximately five hundred years before Christ), rebuilt the city, rebuilt the temple, and restored ceremonial worship of God. They continued to live that way for the next four hundred years. During that time, Persia fell to Greece, and Greece in turn fell to Rome. Rome was ruling that part of the world when Jesus was born.

The ministry of Jesus was preceded by the ministry of His cousin, John the Baptist, who warned the Jews to get ready for the Coming of the Messiah. Jesus was born in Bethlehem, near Jerusalem, in fulfillment of Old Testament prophecy. Then Jesus and His parents, Mary and Joseph, moved back to their hometown in Nazareth, in the northern part of the country, just west of the Sea of

Galilee. There Jesus lived an apparently normal childhood until the age of thirty, when all teachers, by Jewish custom, began their ministry. Jesus began His ministry in Jerusalem and in the surrounding area of Judea. His ministry was highlighted by authoritative teaching and remarkable miracles.

Because of mounting opposition to His ministry on the part of the Jewish religious leaders, Jesus went north to the area around the Sea of Galilee, making Capernaum on the north shore His home base. Much of His three-year ministry was conducted in the area around Capernaum, though many events did not actually take place in Capernaum. Eventually, He returned to Jerusalem and, because of the jealousy of the religious leaders, was soon crucified. Three days later He rose from the dead, and He showed Himself to His disciples several times over the next forty days. Then, with His disciples gathered around Him on the Mount of Olives, just outside Jerusalem, He visibly ascended into heaven.

He had commissioned His disciples to take the new message of salvation through Christ to Jerusalem, Judea, and Samaria (the surrounding regions), and to the uttermost parts of the earth. The church was established in Jerusalem, and the first Christians were Jews. The church there was overseen by Jesus' apostles. The spread of the gospel to the surrounding area and uttermost parts of the earth focused primarily on the apostle Paul, who conducted missionary journeys into areas of Asia Minor and Greece (10). Finally, Paul was arrested and taken to Rome, where he was eventually executed for his faith. There were enough disciples, however, not only in Jerusalem, but also in Asia Minor, Greece, and Rome, that the message not only lived on, but it grew until it became the dominant world religion.

WHAT THE BIBLE TEACHES, IN 1,000 WORDS

When we add all the authors of the Bible and all the books of the Bible together, and boil them down to their irreducible minimum, we learn fundamental truth about ten major subjects. This summary is certainly not all one should know about revealed truth, but it is presented as an introduction, a *getting wet of the feet*, in the pursuit of greater and more indepth knowledge.

We learn that the Bible was revealed by God to man. That is, God made known to mankind, through supernatural means, including visions, dreams direct conversation, etc., what He wanted mankind to know (Hebrews 3:7). Some of this revelation was recorded in the Bible. That information was inspired, meaning that God saw to it that when men wrote down His revelation, they did so without error (2 Peter 1:21). However, people do not readily grasp the deeper spiritual truths of the Scripture. Therefore, the Holy Spirit enables sincere and earnest Christians to understand and embrace the truth of Scripture, illumining their minds to understand the things God has for them (1 Corinthians 2:12). Christians must be diligent students of Scripture, however, if they are to benefit from the Holy Spirit's illumining ministry, studying with an attitude of faith and obedience (2 Timothy 2:15).

In Scripture, we learn that God exists, as seen through nature and through our conscience (Romans 1:18–20). In addition, we learn His characteristics, what He is like. His characteristics are many, but include that He is all-powerful (Job 42:2), present everywhere simultaneously (Psalm 139:8), and knows all things (Psalm 139:4). We learn also that He is holy (Isaiah 5:16), loving (1 John 4:8), and just (Psalm 19:9). God is sovereign and can do whatever He wills (Psalm 135:5, 6) and exists in the Trinity, meaning that there is only one God, but that He exists as three co-equal and co-eternal persons, the same in substance, but distinct in subsistence (Deuteronomy 6:4; 2 Corinthians 13:14).

Jesus of Nazareth was God incarnate, the second member of the Trinity (John 1:10). He was a human (John 1:14), and yet at the same time divine, the only God-man ever to exist. He lived a sinless life, was crucified, and rose again from the dead (Romans 1:4). He is now in heaven, but will return to earth some day to fulfill the plan of God (Titus 2:13).

The Holy Spirit, the third member of the Trinity (2 Corinthians 13:14), is also God, a personal being, not an impersonal force like "school spirit" (Ephesians 4:30). The Holy Spirit plays an instrumental role in each person's salvation, including conviction: revealing to us a need to repent (John 16:8); regeneration: imparting a new spirit and eternal life (Titus 3:5); indwelling: living within us once we are true Christians (Romans 8:9); baptism: placing a believer into the body of Christ (1 Corinthians 12:13); and sealing: guaranteeing the believer's relationship to God (Ephesians 1:13). God wants each of us to serve Him and minister to others, so the Holy Spirit gives each of us special gifts to do so (1 Corinthians 12:4, 11).

Angels are spirit beings who serve God and do His will (Hebrews 1:14). Demons are once-righteous angels who fell, rebelling against God and following Satan (Jude 6). Satan is the highest once-righteous angel who fell, becoming evil and corrupt. He is a real person who oversees demons and seeks to neutralize and overthrow the will of God (1 Peter 5:8). God has given us supernatural defenses to protect us from Satan's attempts to discourage, defeat, and even destroy us. These defenses are called the armor of God (Ephesians 6:13–18).

Humans were created by God as the pinnacle of His creation. We were created in the spiritual, intellectual, emotional, and moral image of God (Genesis 1:27), whose purpose it is to glorify God and enjoy Him forever. Humans have a spiritual, as well as, physical dimension (1 Thessalonians 5:23), and their spirits live forever, either in heaven or in hell (Hebrews 9:27). Man is distinct in God's creation, having capacities exceeding those of the animals (Genesis 1:26).

Sin is the lack of conformity to the moral perfection of God. All humans have been contaminated by sin (1 John 5:17). Adam and Eve, the first humans, were the first to sin. Their sin brought into the world all the pain, evil and suffering, which has been passed down to all other humans, and is so bad that is was called the "Fall" of humanity (Genesis 3:6). We are not sinners because we sin, rather we sin because we are sinners (Ephesians 2:1,3). Because our internal nature has been corrupted, we cannot keep from sinning (Romans 3:23, 6:23), a fact that brings spiritual death to each one.

Salvation is a gift God gives to those who believe (Ephesians 2:8, 9). We are separated from God because of our sin, and when we believe in Jesus and receive Him as our Lord and Savior, God forgives our sin and gives us eternal life (Romans 5:1). The penalty for our sin was paid for by Jesus when He died on the Cross for our sin, which is called the substitutionary death of Christ (1 Peter 3:18). Our spiritual salvation begins when we receive Christ, but our salvation is complete when we die, or when Jesus returns, whichever comes first (Romans 8:23).

The universal church is the totality of all believers in Jesus, from His First Coming to His Second Coming, and is to be the representation of Christ on earth, collectively doing His will (Matthew 16:18). A local church is a local assembly of believers who organize to carry out the ideals of the universal church (1 Corinthians 1:1, 2). A local church is to be led by pastor-teachers, elders, and deacons. Only spiritually mature people are to be given positions of spiritual leadership (1 Timothy 3:2–4, 6, 7). When a person becomes a Christian, he or she becomes a member of the universal church, and should also become committed to a local church, placing him/herself under the spiritual authority of qualified leadership, and becoming involved in mutual ministry to other believers (Hebrews 10:24–25).

As future things begin to unfold, Jesus will return to earth as King to establish righteousness (Matthew 16:27). At two different times and places, God will judge all humanity to confirm their eternal destiny, either in heaven or hell (2 Corinthians 5:10; Revelation 20:15). Then, the old universe will be destroyed and replaced with a new one (Revelation 21:1), and Christians will live with God in glory, joy, and love, forever (Revelation 22:5).

THE MESSAGE OF THE BIBLE

It has been said that the message of the Bible is so simple, the smallest child can understand it, and so deep that the most profound scholar cannot plumb its depths. On its simplest level, the Bible tells us that God created us in His image, and loves us with a love so great we cannot comprehend it. For reasons hidden in the mystery of God's will, humanity sinned against Him. This sin separated all mankind from God, and destined us for an eternity in hell. Yet, because God so loved each one of us, He sent His Son, Jesus, to die in our place. Because He was God, and sinless, the Father is willing to place our sin on Jesus and give Jesus' righteousness to us. He does this when we believe in Jesus as the risen Son of God, and receive Him, or accept Him as our God. This we must do by a simple act of faith. When, in faith, we acknowledge to God that we believe in Jesus and accept Him as our personal God, being willing to turn from our own life to follow Him, God forgives our sin, past, present and future, and gives us eternal life. From that moment, we are destined for heaven as a child of God. God wants us to live for Him while still on earth, so our lives must be committed to following God as best we know how. We discern His will for our lives by reading the Scripture and doing what we find there, as best we can. In addition, we pray and integrate our lives with other committed Christians who can also help us live the life we are now called to. Jesus said the greatest Commandment is to love the Lord our God with all our heart, soul, and mind, and that the second is to love our neighbor as ourselves. This is our task, in its broadest sense, while on earth. When we die, we go to heaven.

If you have come to the point in your life in which you would like to respond to God in this way, tell Him that in the best way you know how. If you would like some guidance, read the following Scriptures, and pray accordingly.

Believe that God created you and loves you, and wants you to have a meaningful life on earth and eternal life with Him in heaven (John 3:16; John 10:10; Ephesians 1:3–8).

2. Tell God that you know that you have sinned and are therefore separated from Him, destined for an eternity in hell, and that you want to saved from your sin and its consequences (Romans 3:23, 6:23; Acts 16:30, 31).

3. Believe that Jesus is the only way our sins can be forgiven, and we can be made right with God (Romans 5:8; John 14:6).

4. Accept Jesus as the Lord of your life, giving yourself to Him to trust and obey Him, primarily by reading Scripture, praying, and becoming involved with other sincere Christians in a local church. Trust that you are truly made right with God through your act of faith in Jesus (John 1:12; Ephesians 2:8, 9; Revelation 3:20).

If you are ready to give your life to Jesus, you might pray something like the following:

> *Father in heaven, I believe in You, and I trust that You love me and want me to have a meaningful life here on earth, and eternal life in heaven. I acknowledge that I have sinned against You. I am prepared to turn from my sin as best I can. Please forgive my sin. I want to be saved from my sin and its terrible consequences. I believe that only through Jesus can my sins be forgiven. I believe in Him, and invite Him to come into my life and be my Savior and Lord. I will live for Him as best I can, trying my best to discern His will for my life through reading Scripture, prayer, and joining a church of sincere Christians who will help me. I know that I will repeatedly fail, but I invite You to come into my life and make me into the kind of person You want me to be, and take me to heaven when I die. Amen.*

If you pray this prayer, meaning it sincerely, then you are now a Christian. Your sins are forgiven. The Bible says that the Holy Spirit comes into your life to help you become what God wants you to be. It is an imperfect and sloppy process. You will often feel that you are taking one step forward and two steps back. But God will be faithful and will help you. Never give up, no matter what. Join a good church of sincere Christians who believe and follow the Bible. That will be the key to your success. You will flounder otherwise. Get a Bible and begin reading it. Don't worry about what you don't understand. There will be much. Just underline and try to follow what you do. The Holy Spirit will gradually enable you to understand more and more.

Also, pray to God. Tell Him the deepest thoughts of your heart. Ask Him to guide you, to help you discern His will for your life, and to bless your life as you live for Him. Learn more about prayer by reading the Bible and by joining with other Christians for prayer.

There are many good preachers on television and the radio, but be sure to compare everything they say with Scripture. There are also some who will lead you astray if you are not careful. There are good books, also. Ask the Lord to guide you to the help your need to grow in Him. You might get *The New Christian's Handbook*, another book I have written, to give you an overview of your new life in Christ, and how to begin growing.

A P P E N D I X
STORY OF THE BIBLE

ERA	FIGURE		STORY LINE SUMMARY
Creation	Adam	Eden	Adam is created by God, but he sins and destroys God's original plan for man.
Patriarch	Abraham	Canaan	Abraham is chosen by God to "father" a people to represent God to the world.
Exodus	Moses	Egypt	Through Moses God delivers the Hebrew people from slavery in Egypt and then gives them the Law.
Conquest	Joshua	Canaan	Joshua leads the conquest of the Promised Land.
Judges	Samson	Canaan	Samson and others were chosen as judges to govern the people for four hundred rebellious years.
Kingdom	David	Israel	David, the greatest king in the new monarchy, is followed by a succession of mostly unrighteous kings, and God eventually judges Israel for her sin, sending her into exile.
Exile	Daniel	Babylonia	Daniel gives leadership and encourages faithfulness among the exiles for the next seventy years.
Return	Ezra	Jerusalem	Ezra leads the people back from exile to rebuild Jerusalem.
Silence	Pharisees	Jerusalem	Pharisees and others entomb the Israelites in legalism for the next four hundred years.

ERA	FIGURE		STORY LINE SUMMARY
Gospels	Jesus	Palestine	Jesus comes in fulfillment of the Old Testament *prophecies* of a savior and offers *salvation* and the true kingdom of God. While some accept Him, most *reject* Him, and He is crucified, buried, and resurrected.
Church	Peter	Jerusalem	Peter, shortly after the *Ascension* of Jesus, is used by God to *establish* the *church*, God's next major plan for man.
Missions	Paul	Roman Empire	Paul *expands* the church into the *Roman* Empire during the next two *decades*.

ARC OF BIBLE HISTORY

TEN GREAT DOCTRINES OF THE BIBLE

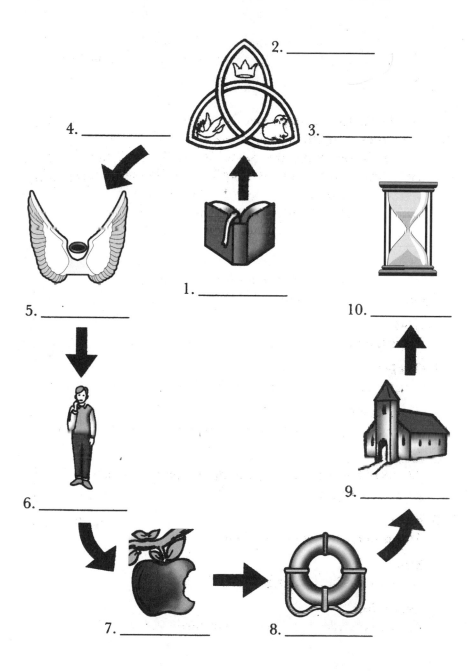

2. _____

4. _____

3. _____

1. _____

5. _____

10. _____

6. _____

9. _____

7. _____

8. _____

Teaching Plan

Introduction

The book *30 Days to Understanding the Bible* is an excellent tool for people who want to learn more about the Bible and its life-transforming message. The book features such learning helps as maps, charts, tables, review exercises, and self-tests to encourage reader interaction with the material in order to increase learning and comprehension.

Group study of *30 Days* adds another dimension to the learning process. In a group, students can interact with the teacher as well as one another to deepen their insights into the nature and purpose of the Bible. The following teaching suggestions are designed to help you lead an effective group study of this important book.

Your students will be expected to read the book on their own. But they will attend the group study to process what they are learning, discuss their ideas with others, clarify the insights and facts to which they are being exposed, and perhaps even celebrate with one another the blessings which come with greater understanding of God's Word.

Preview of the Study

The thirty chapters of *30 Days to Understanding the Bible* will be covered in the following thirteen sessions:

✓ Session 1: *wk 1 + 2*	Structure of the Bible, Old Testament Geography, and Historical Books (Chs. 1—3)
✓ Session 2: *wk 3*	The Old Testament Story, Creation—Conquest (Chs. 4—7)
✓ Session 3: *wk 4*	The Old Testament Story, Judges—Silence (Chs. 8—12)
Session 4:	Poetical and Prophetical Books (Chs. 13 and 14)
Session 5:	New Testament Geography and Structure (Ch. 15)
Session 6:	Gospel/Church Eras (Chs. 16 and 17)
Session 7:	Missions Era/Epistles (Chs. 18 and 19)

Session 8:	Foundations of Christian Belief (Chs. 20 and 21)
Session 9:	God and His Son (Chs. 22 and 23)
Session 10:	The Holy Spirit and Angels (Chs. 24 and 25)
Session 11:	Man and Sin (Chs. 26 and 27)
Session 12:	Salvation and the Church (Chs. 28 and 29)
Session 13:	The Doctrine of Future Things (Ch. 30)

REPRODUCIBLE IMAGES FOR TEACHING

At the back of this book (see pp. 301–330) you will find images, maps, and charts which may be enlarged on a copy machine and converted into transparencies for use on an overhead projector. They are also available for download from www.thomasnelson.com/30days for use in electronic presentations. Picked up from various places throughout this book, these images will be used in various sessions throughout this study. For your convenience, here's a complete list of these images. (*Details on how to use them appear in the individual session plans below.*)

- Old Testament Books/New Testament Books
- The Three Kinds of Books in the Old Testament
- The Three Kinds of Books in the New Testament
- Work Map: Locations of the Old Testament
- Map: State of Texas/Land of the Bible
- Overview of Old Testament History
- Arc of Bible History
- Bodies of Water in the Gospels
- The Geography of Acts
- Overview of New Testament History
- Time Line of the New Testament
- Map of Palestine
- Map of the New Testament World
- Ten Great Doctrines of the Bible
- Four Major Subdivisions of the Doctrine of the Bible
- Four Major Subdivisions of the Doctrine of God
- Four Major Subdivisions of the Doctrine of Christ

- Four Major Subdivisions of the Doctrine of the Holy Spirit
- Four Major Subdivisions of the Doctrine of Angels
- Four Major Subdivisions of the Doctrine of Man
- Four Major Subdivisions of the Doctrine of Sin
- Four Major Subdivisions of the Doctrine of Salvation
- Four Major Subdivisions of the Doctrine of the Church
- Four Major Subdivisions of the Doctrine of Future Things
- Review of Ten Great Doctrines and Their Subdivisions

GENERAL PREPARATION FOR THE STUDY

In order to lead students in this study of the Bible, you must be well prepared yourself. Here are some practical steps you can take to make sure you are ready before the time for Session 1 rolls around.

1. Read this book thoroughly at least once. Take time to complete the written exercises in the book. This will give you a good idea of the challenges and rewards your students will face in the study of the material.

2. Look over the teaching plans for all thirteen sessions. Note especially those sessions that suggest that you give advance assignments to students. Make a note on the students whom you will ask to do these extra tasks. Begin now to enlist students in advance for these assignments.

3. Pull together a selection of reference books that might be helpful to students who agree to do these extra assignments. Bible dictionaries, Bible handbooks, and books which overview the entire Bible should be especially helpful.

4. Prepare the room by arranging the chairs in circular fashion in order to generate dialogue and discussion among the students. Collect equipment and learning aids you will need—computer, television, overhead projector, chalkboard or poster board, pencils or pens, felt-tip pens, etc.

5. Pray that the Lord will bless your teaching and that the students will be open and receptive to truths and insights presented during this study.

6. Remember, these lesson outlines are guides, not straightjackets. Feel free to amend them so they meet your needs. You may have to add or subtract material based on your students' previous knowledge or the amount of time you have. You may want to cover the material in six sessions or sixteen rather than thirteen. The procedures offered here assume a class session of 45 minutes to one hour.

NOTE: Before the first class, have the students read Chapters 1—3, but they should not fill in the blanks in their books.

SESSION 1: STRUCTURE OF THE BIBLE, OLD TESTAMENT GEOGRAPHY, AND HISTORICAL BOOKS

Overview: This session covers the material in Chapters 1—3.

Before the Session

1. Prepare the following items from the back of this book or the website for display during this session:

- Old Testament/New Testament Books
- The Three Kinds of Books in the Old Testament
- The Three Kinds of Books in the New Testament
- Work Map: Locations of the Old Testament
- Map: State of Texas/Land of the Bible
- Overview of Old Testament History

2. Review Chapters 1—3 to call to mind the content to be covered in this session. Be sure to complete all the self-tests, writing the answers to the questions in your book.

3. Read carefully the article "The Summary of the Bible," while looking at the "Geography of the Old Testament" map to be sure you have the big picture of the story in your mind.

4. Prepare a poster with the titles of all thirteen sessions of this study (see "Preview of the Study" above). Place this poster in a prominent place in the room. Leave this poster up throughout the study as a visible reminder to the students of the progress they are making. You might even place a check mark on each session as it is completed, and remind them at the beginning of each session of the lessons they have already completed.

During the Session

1. Open with prayer that this will be a profitable and encouraging study for everyone.

2. As an icebreaker, have the students break into pairs (assuming they do not know each other), introduce themselves to one another and chat for two or three minutes. Then ask them to introduce their partners to the rest of the group, telling their name and other information such as family, employment, hobbies, etc.

3. Direct the students' attention to the wall poster with an outline of all thirteen sessions of the study, commenting on the scope of this challenging learning opportunity. Remind students that they will be expected to complete the reading for each session in their books before they come to class, but they will not fill in the blanks. This will be done in class after a review of the material. If they want to take the quiz at home when they read the chapter, have them write the answers on another sheet of paper.

4. Display the "Old Testament Books/New Testament Books" chart. Review the information, then have them close their books and ask them how many books are in the Old Testament, in the New Testament, and the whole Bible.

Finally, have them write the answers in their books.

NOTE: This pattern of orally drilling the students until they seem to know the answers, then having them fill in the blanks in their books, will be used frequently throughout the book

5. Display the "The Three Kinds of Books in the Old Testament" chart, followed by "The Three Kinds of Books in the New Testament." Review the information on these charts, then drill the students until they can give you the responses readily. Then, have them complete the self-tests on pages 19–20. Remind them that they will learn more about these books and the categories of literature to which they belong in later sessions of this study.

6. Have one or more persons read aloud "The Summary of the Bible." On the map of the Old Testament, draw the arrows for each number in the story that show the movement of the story.

7. Display the "State of Texas/Land of the Bible" map. Explain that the entire territory known as the "Old Testament World" is approximately the same size as the state of Texas. Most students are

surprised to learn that the Old Testament world was no larger than this. Ask, "How does this compare with what you had previously thought about the size of the Old Testament world?"

8. Display the "Work Map: Locations of the Old Testament." Point out the locations A through G, and 1–8 on this map, commenting briefly on the significance of each. Then point at each of these places again, asking the students to provide the correct name. Next, have the students do the same for their partners, and the partners for the students. Finally, ask them to complete the self-test.

9. Display the "Overview of Old Testament History," explaining that this chart is a convenient summary of all the material covered in Chapter 3 in their books. More than 2,000 years of biblical history are represented by this chart.

Cover the chart so that none of the information shows. Then ask students to search Chapter 3 in their books and find the following information. As they locate and call out the information, uncover it:

- The nine eras of Old Testament history
- The major figure or biblical personality of each era
- The primary geographic location of the events in these nine different eras
- The story lines which summarize these nine eras, their personalities, and their locations.

10. If time permits, divide the students into teams of two. Ask them to work together to complete the remaining self-tests in Chapters 1—3. If time does not permit, you can tell them the answers to complete all the remaining self-tests.

11. Close with prayer.

Looking Ahead to the Next Session

Remind the students that the next session will cover Chapters 4—7. They should read the material, but not fill in the blanks in their books. This will be done in class.

SESSION 2: THE OLD TESTAMENT STORY
(CREATION—CONQUEST)

Overview: This session covers the material in Chapters 4—7.

Before the Session

1. Prepare the following items from the back of this book or the website for display during this session:

- Overview of Old Testament History
- Arc of Bible History

2. Gather materials needed to create a "map" on the floor, so that as you review the Old Testament story, Creation—Conquest, you can point/walk to the place on the floor map where the event occurred. Use the Old Testament Work Map as your guide. The floor map only needs to approximate the accuracy of a real map, especially since you can display the real map as you lay out the floor map. You will need:

- Cord/string/rope long enough to use as the coastline for the Mediterranean Sea.
- Shorter cord/string/rope for the Jordan, Tigris, and Euphrates Rivers.
- Small paperback book (or anything else) to represent the Sea of Galilee.
- Two larger books (or anything else) to represent the Dead Sea.
- Styrofoam/plastic cups on which you can, with a felt-tip marker, write the names of cities, countries, etc.

Make the map as large as feasible for your room. Then, as you tell the story, you can walk or point to the appropriate place on the floor map.

3. Prepare a 15–30 minute (depending on how long your session is) presentation of the story of the Old Testament, Creation—Conquest. Follow the story in the book. Be sure to highlight the information called for in the self-test material. It is desirable for you to supplement the book material with your own knowledge and to be able to answer questions. If you need help preparing, consult a Bible handbook, Bible atlas, and other material. *Reader's Digest* has published *Great People of the Bible and How They Lived*, which can also

be a good source of historical, geographical, and cultural information (though you may not always agree with some of their theological or spiritual comments).

4. Read Chapters 4—7 and complete the self-tests and learning exercises. Remember, a good teacher should always be at least a step or two ahead of his or her students!

During the Session

1. Open with prayer for God's guidance and blessing during this session.

2. As a review for students, display the "Overview of Old Testament History," which you used last session. Lead them to identify the nine eras of Old Testament history.

3. Display the "Arc of Bible History," pointing out that the first four eras of Old Testament history (Creation—Conquest) are represented by the first four icons on the chart (the next five represent the last five eras in Old Testament history, and the final three icons represent New Testament history). Point to each icon and ask the students to name these four eras. Ask the students to quiz each other in teams of two until they readily identify the era by pointing to the icon. They can use their books for this review.

4. Talk through the history of Creation—Conquest, walking through the map as you do. After you have gone through it indepth once, go through it quickly a time or two as review. After you have finished with the events in a given era, point to the icon on the "Arc of Bible History" to reinforce the era with the events.

5. If time permits, have the partners help each other as they fill in all the self-test material. If time does not permit, talk them through the answers yourself.

6. Close with a prayer of thanksgiving for the peole of Old Testament times who obeyed God and passed His message on to succeeding generations, and who helped us understand how to live by faith.

Looking Ahead to the Next Session

Remind the students to read Chapters 8—12 before the next session.

SESSION 3: THE OLD TESTAMENT STORY
(CONQUEST—SILENCE)

Overview: This session covers the material in Chapters 8—12.

Before the Session

Make the same preparations for this session (Conquest—Silence, Chapters 8—12) as you did for the last session.

During the Session

Use exactly the same procedures for this session as you did for the last session, but relating the information on Conquest—Silence, found in Chapters 8—12.

Looking Ahead to the Next Session

Remind the students to read Chapters 13 and 14 before the next session.

SESSION 4: POETICAL BOOKS AND PROPHETICAL BOOKS

Overview: This session covers the material in Chapters 13 and 14.

Before the Session

1. Prepare the following items from the back of this book or the website for display during this session:

- The Three Kinds of Books in the Old Testament
- Work Map: Locations of the Old Testament

2. Enlist a student in your class to do research on "The Poetic Books of the Old Testament" and to be prepared to present a five-minute report on this topic during Session 4. (If this does not fit your circumstances, prepare the report yourself.)

3. Enlist another student to do research on "The Prophets of the Old Testament" and to be prepared to present a five-minute report on this topic during Session 4 (or do it yourself).

4. Review Chapters 13 and 14 to call to mind the content to be covered in Session 4. Be sure to complete the self-tests on pages 105 and 110, writing the answers to these questions in your book.

5. Enlist a student to read a short psalm from the Book of Psalms and to lead the class in prayer at the beginning of the session, if appropriate. If your class is geared to seekers or young/new Christians, be cautious of embarrassing them.

During the Session

1. Call on the student whom you have enlisted to read a short psalm and lead the class in prayer.

2. Remind the students that this psalm read at the beginning of the class is from the Book of Psalms—one of the great poetic books of the Old Testament. Then state that you will be studying the poetic and prophetic books of the Old Testament during this session.

3. Display "The Three Kinds of Books in the Old Testament" chart to show that poetic books make up one of the major categories of Old Testament literature.

4. Call on the student whom you have enlisted to give the report on "The Poetic Books of the Old Testament." Ask the other students to open their books to pages 104–105 while this report is being presented and to compare the student report with this printed information. They might jot down in the margins of their books on these pages any important information covered by the student report.

5. After the student report, drill the students on the self-test. Then have them review the material with their partner. Finally, let the students complete the self-test on page 105.

6. Display "The Three Kinds of Books in the Old Testament" transparency again. Ask which of these books are known as the *major prophets* and which are called the *minor prophets*. What do these two terms mean—*major prophets* and *minor prophets*?

7. Call on the student whom you have enlisted to give a report on "The Prophets of the Old Testament." Then ask the class to turn to the information on "Structure of the Prophetical Books" (pp. 109–110). Point out that the prophetical books were addressed to many different regions of the Old Testament world under many different situations and conditions.

8. Display the "Map: Locations of the Old Testament." Ask students to locate on this map the different nations and regions to which the prophetical books of the Old Testament were addressed.

9. Drill the students on the self-test for the prophetical books. Then have them review with their partners. Finally, have them complete the self-test on page 110.

10. Ask a student to lead the closing prayer, if appropriate, expressing special thanks for the poetic and prophetic books of the Old Testament. If your students are unaccustomed to praying in public, close with prayer yourself.

Looking Ahead to the Next Session

1. Remind the class to read Chapter 15 of their books before the next class meeting—Session 5.

SESSION 5: NEW TESTAMENT GEOGRAPHY AND STRUCTURE

Overview: This session covers the material in Chapter 15.

Before the Session

1. Prepare the following items from the back of this book or the website for display during this session:

- Bodies of Water in the Gospels
- The Geography of Acts
- Overview of New Testament History
- Arc of Bible History

2. Review Chapter 15 to call to mind the content to be covered in this session. Be sure to complete the self-test on page 120, writing the answers in the blanks in your book.

3. Pray for the Holy Spirit's guidance as you prepare to lead the class in this important session on an introduction to the New Testament.

During the Session

1. Begin with a prayer of thanks to God for the two grand divisions of the Bible—the Old Testament and the New Testament. Ask for God's insight and guidance in this introductory study on the New Testament.

2. Call attention to the poster with titles of all thirteen sessions of this study of the Bible. Remind the students that you have now

completed all sessions on the Old Testament and that this session marks the beginning of your studies of the New Testament. Use the following questions to generate interest and discussion about the New Testament and its relationship to the Old Testament.

- What's your favorite section of the Bible—the Old Testament or the New Testament? Why?
- What's the major difference between the Old Testament and the New Testament?
- Which is more important—the Old Testament or the New Testament?
- Which is easier to understand—the Old Testament or the New Testament?

3. Display the "Bodies of Water in the Gospels," asking students to identify these bodies of water in the New Testament world and to write these names in their books (p. 117).

4. Ask the students to open their books to pages 119–120 while you display "The Geography of Acts." Mention each of these sites and its significance, pointing out its location on the transparency. Then divide the class into teams of two and let them work together on learning these names and their locations, completing the blank map on page 121 of their books.

5. Display the "Overview of New Testament History." Then flash the "Overview of Old Testament History" briefly, followed by the "Overview of New Testament History." Note that Old Testament history features nine different eras covering about 2,000 years, while New Testament history has only three different eras covering about 100 years. Reinforce this truth by displaying the "Arc of Bible History," which shows all twelve eras of biblical history together.

6. Ask the students to turn to page 122 in their books. Then lead them to complete the exercises on page 122 and 124–125 and to write the answers in their books. Take time to answer questions or provide information as needed to broaden their understanding about the geography and structure of the New Testament.

7. Close with prayer.

Looking Ahead to the Next Session

1. Remind the class to read Chapters 16 and 17 of their books before the next class—Session 6.

SESSION 6: GOSPEL/CHURCH ERAS

Overview: This session covers the material in Chapters 16 and 17.

Before the Session

1. Prepare the map of Palestine from the back of this book or the website and have it ready to display during this session.

2. Review Chapters 16 and 17 to call to mind the content to be covered in this session. Be sure to complete the self-tests, writing the answers to these questions in your book.

3. Gather materials needed for a floor map of the New Testament area.

4. Write the following outline on the chalkboard or a large sheet of poster paper, leaving adequate space after each point for writing in major events from the life of Jesus:

MAJOR EVENTS IN JESUS' LIFE

1. Early Life: Childhood to Baptism

2. Early Ministry: Initial Acceptance

3. Later Ministry: Growing Rejection

4. Death and Resurrection: Final Rejection

Note that this outline comes from pages 129–130 of the book.

During the Session

1. Lead in a prayer of thanksgiving for the life and ministry of Jesus and His saving power, and ask for His blessings on the session.

2. Remind the students that today's study will focus on the life and ministry of Jesus and the beginning of the church. Point out that Jesus' ministry lasted only about three years and it was conducted in an area only about thirty miles wide by ninety miles long.

3. Display the the map of Palestine, pointing out the relatively small size of Palestine. Ask the students to identify in the life of Jesus the significance of each of these five places on the map:

- Bethlehem
- Egypt
- Nazareth
- Capernaum
- Jerusalem

4. Using the same materials you used for the Old Testament, lay out a map of the New Testament area on the floor of the room. Direct the students' attention to the outline, "Major Events in Jesus' Life," which you have posted in the room. Ask them to help you fill in this outline by recalling major events in His life and ministry under each point on the outline. Write these events on the outline as they are recalled by the class. As they are identified, trace the geographical movement on the floor map. Here are a few major events, just in case you don't get any help from your students (Be sure you know where all these events took place):

(1) Early Life
      Birth in Bethlehem
      Flight into Egypt
      Presentation as an infant in the temple
      Discussion with learned scholars in the temple
(2) Early Ministry: Acceptance
      Temptations in the wilderness
      Miracles of healing
      Sermon on the Mount
      Calling of His disciples
(3) Later Ministry: Rejection
      Clash with Pharisees and Sadducees
      Withdrawal with His disciples
      Teaching His disciples about His forthcoming death
      Peter's confession at Caesarea–Philippi

(4) Death and Resurrection
  Triumphal entry into Jerusalem
  Last Supper with His disciples
  Agonizing prayer in the Garden of Gethsemane
  Crucifixion
  Resurrection
  Post-resurrection appearances

5. Ask the students to turn to page 130 in their books and to review with their partner before they complete the self-test and other exercises.

6. Display the "Map of Palestine" again and show on this map how the church spread from Jerusalem to Judea to Samaria after Jesus' Ascension, in accordance with the promise and prediction of Jesus. Write "Judea" and "Samaria" on the map. Explain that this stage of the growth of the church is described in chapters 1—12 of the Book of Acts.

7. Close with a prayer of thanks for Jesus, the gospel, and the church.

Looking Ahead to the Next Session

1. Remind the class to read the text and complete the exercises in Chapters 18 and 19 of their books before the next meeting—Session 7.

SESSION 7: MISSIONS ERA/EPISTLES

Overview: This session covers the material in Chapters 18 and 19.

Before the Session

1. Prepare the following items from the back of this book or the website for display during this session:

- Time Line of the New Testament
- Map of the New Testament World

2. Enlist two students to research and prepare two different five-minute reports on the apostle Paul for presentation during Session 7. One report should focus on "The Life and Missionary Travels of

Paul," while the other should cover "The Epistles and Theological Contribution of Paul." If you have no volunteers, prepare them yourself.

3. Review Chapters 18 and 19 to call to mind the content to be covered in this session. Be sure to complete the self-tests.

During the Session

1. Begin the class with prayer, asking the Holy Spirit to direct the class during the session as you focus on the exciting years of the expansion of the early church.

2. Display the "Map of the New Testament World." Ask the students to open their books to page 143. Explain that the person who took the lead in planting churches throughout the New Testament world during the first Christian century was the apostle Paul. Page 143 in their books gives an outline of the missionary travels of this great "apostle to the Gentiles."

3. Introduce the student whom you have enlisted to give a report on "The Life and Missionary Travels of Paul." Ask the other students to take notes during this presentation, comparing the facts presented with the outline of Paul's travels on page 143 in their books. After this presentation, generate additional discussion on Paul with questions such as these:

- Why do you think Paul became the great "apostle to the Gentiles"? How was he uniquely qualified for his role as the first great missionary of Christianity?
- How did Paul support himself during his missionary travels?
- Who were some of the key helpers and companions who assisted Paul in his work?

4. After this discussion, ask students to turn to page 144 in their books and review with their partners before they complete the self-test on the major events in Paul's life.

5. Display the "Time Line of the New Testament" transparency. Ask the students to turn to page 150 in their books. Ask them to identify the twenty-year period during which the epistles of Paul were written by comparing these epistles with the time line. Point

out that Paul was more than a great missionary in early Christianity; he was also a great theologian and letter writer who wrote thirteen of the twenty-seven books of the New Testament.

6. Ask the students to open their books to pages 151–153, which discuss Paul's epistles to churches and individuals. Then introduce the student whom you have enlisted to present a report on "The Epistles and Theological Contribution of Paul." Ask them to fill in the blanks in their books regarding Paul's epistles as they listen to the presentation on this subject.

7. Refer the students to the information about the general epistles on pages 153–154 of their books. Lead a discussion of these books, helping them to fill in the blanks in their books with the missing information about these epistles.

8. Call on a student, if appropriate, to close with a prayer of thanksgiving for the apostle Paul and his contribution to God's kingdom.

SESSION 8: FOUNDATIONS OF CHRISTIAN BELIEF

Overview: This session covers the material in Chapters 20 and 21.

Before the Session

1. Prepare the following items from the back of this book or the website for display during this session:

- Ten Great Doctrines of the Bible
- Four Major Subdivisions of the Doctrine of the Bible

2. Review Chapters 20 and 21 in the book to call to mind the content to be covered in this session. Be sure to complete the review on pages 167–168 and the self-test on page 176, writing the answers to these questions in your book.

3. Locate and read the Bible passages that relate to the four major subdivisions of the Bible: Hebrews 3:7; 2 Peter 1:21; 1 Corinthians 2:12; and 2 Timothy 2:15. Read these passages in several translations and be prepared to discuss them with the students.

4. List the ten great doctrines of the Bible on the chalkboard or place them on poster board in a prominent position in the room.

During the Session

1. Open with prayer that this will be a profitable and rewarding learning experience for all students.

2. Display the "Ten Great Doctrines of the Bible." Explain that the final six sessions of the study will focus on these ten major doctrines.

3. Direct the students' attention to the ten major doctrines which you have listed on the chalkboard or poster board. Ask them to match these words with the appropriate logos on the "Ten Great Doctrines" chart. Write these words in the appropriate spaces as they are matched correctly by the students.

4. After all the logos and words have been matched correctly, generate discussion on these doctrines by asking questions such as these:

- Of these ten doctrines, which is most important, in your opinion?
- Why do you think the Bible is listed as the first of these ten doctrines?
- Why are God, Christ, and the Holy Spirit grouped together on this transparency?

5. Display the "Four Major Subdivisions of the Bible." Explain that these are important words about the Bible—revelation, inspiration, illumination, and interpretation—which every Christian needs to understand.

6. Call on one student to read aloud Hebrews 3:7, a second to read 2 Peter 1:21, a third to read 1 Corinthians 2:12, and a fourth to read 2 Timothy 3:15. Ask the other students to follow in their Bibles as these are being read. Then ask them to match these Bible verses with the "Four Major Subdivisions of the Bible" transparency.

7. Have the students turn to pages 175 and 176 in their books and complete the review and self-test exercises on the Bible.

8. Close with a prayer of thanksgiving for these ten great doctrines of the Christian faith, especially the Bible and its influence in the lives of believers.

Looking Ahead to the Next Session

1. Remind the class to read the text and complete the learning exercises in Chapters 22 and 23 of their books before the next class session—Session 9.

SESSION 9: GOD AND HIS SON

Overview: This session covers the material in Chapters 22 and 23.

Before the Session

1. Prepare the following items from the back of this book or the website for display during this session:

- Ten Great Doctrines of the Bible
- Four Major Subdivisions of the Doctrine of God
- Four Major Subdivisions of the Doctrine of Christ

2. Review Chapters 22 and 23 to call to mind the content to be covered in this session. Be sure to complete the self-tests on pages 184–185 and 193, writing the answers to these questions in your book.

3. Ask a student in advance to do some research on the doctrine of God and to be prepared to bring a five-minute report on this subject during the session. A good one-volume Bible dictionary should have an article on this subject. Ask him or her to concentrate specifically on the names and attributes of God in this report.

During the Session

1. Call on a student to lead in prayer for the Holy Spirit's guidance during this session.

2. Refer the students to the poster with the outline of this thirteen-session study, reminding them that you will be studying about God and His Son Jesus during this session.

3. Display the "Ten Great Doctrines of the Bible," leading the students to review and recall these ten major doctrines. Point to the triangle at the top and remind them that they will be studying about two persons of the Trinity during this session—God and His Son.

4. Display the "Four Major Subdivisions of the Doctrine of God." Lecture briefly on the "existence," "sovereignty," and "trinity" points of this chart. Then introduce the student whom you enlisted

in advance to present a brief report on the names and attributes of God. After the report, help the students to clarify their thinking by asking questions like these and leading them in a general discussion:

- What do we mean by the "attributes" of God?
- What do we mean when we say that God is "sovereign"?
- How do we know that God exists?

5. Break the students into several small groups. Have half the small groups work on the "divine attributes" section in their books (pp. 183, 184), while the other groups work on the "personal attributes" section (p. 184). Ask them to look up all the Scriptures mentioned and discuss these in their small groups, writing in the answers in their books.

6. Display the "Four Major Subdivisions of the Doctrine of Christ." Break the class into four smaller groups. Group 1 should search their Bibles for evidence of the deity of Christ; while group 2 should search for evidence of His humanity; group 3, His Resurrection; and group 4, His return. If time permits, have each group give a brief report on its findings to the rest of the class.

7. Working individually, the students should complete the self-tests in their books on God (pp. 184–185) and Christ (p. 193).

8. Close with prayer that truths which you have discovered about God and Christ will provide guidance and direction for daily living for every member of the class.

Looking Ahead to the Next Session

1. Remind the class to read the text and complete the learning exercises in Chapters 24 and 25 of their books before the next class session.

2. Ask the students during the time before the next session to be on the lookout for "angel evidence"—articles in newspapers and magazines about angels, books on angels in bookstores, testimonies from people who claim to have experienced encounters with angels, etc. The class will discuss this "angel evidence" in Session 10.

SESSION 10: THE HOLY SPIRIT AND ANGELS

Overview: This session covers the material in Chapters 24 and 25.

Before the Session

1. Prepare the following items from the back of this book or the website for display during this session:

- Ten Great Doctrines of the Bible
- Four Major Subdivisions of the Doctrine of the Holy Spirit
- Four Major Subdivisions of the Doctrine of Angels

2. Review Chapters 24 and 25 to call to mind the content to be covered in this session. Be sure to complete the self-tests on pages 203 and 213–214, writing the answers to these questions in your book.

During the Session

1. Begin with a prayer of thanks for the truths and insights you are learning about the great doctrines of the Christian faith.

2. To make sure the students are reading the material and completing the exercises in their books, call for the answers to the self-tests on pages 203 and 213–214. Remind the class that they should be completing the exercises *before* the class sessions.

3. Display the "Ten Great Doctrines of the Bible" and lead the class to identify the three great truths which you have already studied—the Bible, God, and His Son. Remind them that you will be studying the third person of the Trinity—the Holy Spirit—as well as the doctrine of angels during this session.

4. Display the "Four Great Subdivisions of the Doctrine of the Holy Spirit." Lecture briefly on the meaning of "personality" and "deity" on this transparency. Then ask the students to search their books for the interpretation of the symbol of two baby cribs, representing "salvation." When the students find this information and call it out, write this acrostic on the chalkboard:

C-onviction
R-egeneration
I-ndwelling
B-aptism
S-ealing

5. Ask a student to read aloud 1 Corinthians 12:4, 11—one of the classic passages in the New Testament about spiritual gifts given to believers by the Holy Spirit. Ask what spiritual gifts are necessary for the proper functioning of a church.

6. Display the "Four Major Subdivisions of the Doctrine of Angels." Lead the class in a general discussion of the "angel evidence" in our contemporary culture, drawing from their observations of this phenomenon during the past week. Ask why there is a fascination with angels in our society. Do some people have a false view of who angels are and what they do? Ask them to find the biblical definition of angels in their books (p. 209 beside the angel logo).

7. Refer the students to the logos of demons and Satan on the transparency. Ask, Why are *demons* and *Satan* included in this discussion of *angels*? Then ask them to find the three passages of Scripture in their books that represent the protection or defense available to Christians in their fight against Satan. As these passages are discovered (pp. 213–214), write them on the chalkboard:

- 1 Peter 5:8
- Ephesians 6:13
- James 4:7

8. Ask a student to close with prayer, thanking God for His provision of the Holy Spirit and angels for the guidance and protection of believers.

Looking Ahead to the Next Session

1. Remind the class to read the text and complete the learning exercises in Chapters 26 and 27 of their books before the next class session.

SESSION 11: MAN AND SIN

Overview: This session covers the material in Chapters 26 and 27.

Before the Session

1. Prepare the following items from the back of this book or the website for display during this session:

- Ten Great Doctrines of the Bible
- Four Major Subdivisions of the Doctrine of Man
- Four Major Subdivisions of the Doctrine of Sin

2. Review Chapters 26 and 27 to call to mind the content to be covered in this session. Be sure to complete the self-tests on pages 222 and 230–231, writing the answers to these questions in your book.

During the Session

1. Begin with a prayer for God's guidance during this session.

2. Display the "Four Major Subdivisions of the Doctrine of Man." Lecture briefly on the high points of this doctrine, drawing from the material on pages 218–220 of the book.

3. Point out that the doctrine of man is related closely to another major doctrine of the Christian faith—man's sin. Display the "Four Major Subdivisions of the Doctrine of Sin." Lecture briefly on this doctrine, drawing from the material on pages 226–229 of the book.

4. Display the "Ten Great Doctrines of the Bible."

5. Divide the class into several smaller groups, with three or four people in each group. Inform them that they will work together as small groups during the remainder of this session. They will search the Bible together to find evidence of the sinful nature of man and how God deals with sin. They will also work together to review all the great doctrines they have studied so far, completing the review exercise on pages 224–225 of their books. In their groups, they should discuss everything they have studied so far, clarifying their thoughts with one another and turning to previous sections of their books to find needed information. Make yourself available to all groups as a resource person to help them in this review process.

6. After the small groups have concluded their work, lead the class in a general discussion of the doctrines of man and sin, supplementing their ideas, as needed, with additional information. Answer their questions about any doctrine they have studied up to this point.

7. Call on a member of the class to lead in a prayer of thanks for this student-to-student sharing session.

Looking Ahead to the Next Session

1. Remind the class to read the text and complete the learning exercises in Chapters 28 and 29 of their books before the next class session.

SESSION 12: SALVATION AND THE CHURCH

Overview: This session covers the material in Chapters 8 and 9.

Before the Session

1. Prepare the following items from the back of this book or the website for display during this session:

- Four Major Subdivisions of the Doctrine of Salvation
- Four Major Subdivisions of the Doctrine of the Church

2. Review Chapters 28 and 29 to call to mind the content to be covered in this session. Be sure to complete the self-tests on pages 239 and 248–249, writing the answers to these questions in your book.

3. Write the following heading on the chalkboard or a piece of poster board:

THREE FALSE BELIEFS ON HOW TO GET TO HEAVEN

Be prepared to list these false beliefs as they are discovered by students. (See p. 232 in the book.)

4. Make copies of the following fill-in-the-blanks exercise for distribution to students during this session. (You will find these statements on pages 241–242 and 244–245 of the book.)

IMPORTANT FACTS ABOUT THE CHURCH

1. The church is not a building, but _____.
2. The church began on the _____.
3. Augustine said: "_____."
4. The universal church is also called the _____.
5. Every believer should be a part of a _____.

6. Only _____ are to be given high positions of spiritual leadership in the church.

7. The universal church is to be the _____

_____, collectively doing His will.

During the Session

1. Remind the students that the doctrine of sin, which you discussed during Session 11, leads logically to the doctrine of salvation. God's provision of salvation is necessary because of our sin.

2. Refer the students to the heading on the chalkboard, THREE FALSE BELIEFS ON HOW TO GET TO HEAVEN. Ask them to find these three false beliefs in the assigned reading for this session (p. 232). Write them under the heading as they are discovered and called out.

3. Display the "Four Major Subdivisions of the Doctrine of Salvation." Ask for some authentic truths about salvation. Guide the class to highlight the truths about salvation discussed on pages 235–237 of their books.

4. Display the "Four Major Subdivisions of the Doctrine of the Church." Distribute the fill-in-the-blanks exercise, "Important Facts about the Church." Give the students about five to ten minutes to find the answers to these questions in their books, then lead a general discussion of these truths and insights about the church.

Looking Ahead to the Next Session

1. Remind the class to read the text and complete the learning exercises in Chapter 30 of their books before the next class session. Ask them to be sure to complete the review of all ten major doctrines on pp. 259–261, since you will spend some time in Session 13 reviewing what you have learned.

SESSION 13: THE DOCTRINE OF FUTURE THINGS

Overview: This session covers the material in Chapter 30.

Before the Session

1. Make transparencies of the following items from the back of this book and have them ready to display on an overhead projector during the session:

- Ten Great Doctrines of the Bible
- Four Major Subdivisions of the Doctrine of Future Things
- Review of Ten Great Doctrines and Their Subdivisions

2. Review Chapter 30 to call to mind the content to be covered in this session. Be sure to complete the self-test on page 258, writing the answers to these questions in your book.

3. Enlist four students in advance to give brief reports on the four major subdivisions of the doctrine of future things: (1) return, (2) judgment, (3) universe, and (4) eternity.

During the Session

1. Call on a student to lead in prayer.

2. Display the "Four Major Subdivisions of the Doctrine of Future Things." Then introduce the four students who have agreed to bring brief reports on these four subdivisions. Follow up with a general discussion of the central Scriptures that support these points and the meaning of these truths for Christian believers.

3. Display the "Ten Great Doctrines of the Bible" and lead the students to name these ten doctrines by matching them with the appropriate logos.

4. Ask the students to open their books to the more detailed review of these major doctrines on pages 259–261 of their books. Display the "Review of Ten Great Doctrines and Their Subdivisions." With their books closed (if possible) and the review in place, lead them to complete each subpoint by naming it out loud as you point to each line on the chart.

5. Lead the class in a general discussion of truths they remember about each doctrine. List these on the chalkboard as they are called out.

6. Close with a prayer of thanksgiving for these ten great doctrines of the Bible and their meaning in the lives of believers.

REPRODUCIBLE IMAGES FOR TEACHING

On the following pages are images designed for use as teaching aids. They are suitable for copying onto overhead projection cells or scanning for use in Power Point© presentations. They are also available for downloading for electronic presentations from www.thomas-nelson.com/30days. Suggestions for using each of these masters are included in the Teaching Plan on pages 275–300. In each instance they are identified by the title of the master. You probably will want to prepare all the presentation aids before you begin the first session.

Because this book (and therefore the masters which follow) is smaller than a standard sheet of typing paper, you may wish to enlarge the images on your copy machine or scanner by as much as 120 percent.

Old Testament Books

Genesis	2 Chronicles	Daniel
Exodus	Ezra	Hosea
Leviticus	Nehemiah	Joel
Numbers	Esther	Amos
Deuteronomy	Job	Obadiah
Joshua	Psalms	Jonah
Judges	Proverbs	Micah
Ruth	Ecclesiastes	Nahum
1 Samuel	Song of Solomon	Habakkuk
2 Samuel	Isaiah	Zephaniah
1 Kings	Jeremiah	Haggai
2 Kings	Lamentations	Zechariah
1 Chronicles	Ezekiel	Malachi

New Testament Books

Matthew	Ephesians	Hebrews
Mark	Philippians	James
Luke	Colossians	1 Peter
John	1 Thessalonians	2 Peter
Acts	2 Thessalonians	1 John
Romans	1 Timothy	2 John
1 Corinthians	2 Timothy	3 John
2 Corinthians	Titus	Jude
Galatians	Philemon	Revelation

The Three Kinds of Books in the Old Testament

Historical	*Poetical*	*Prophetical*
Genesis	Job	Isaiah
Exodus	Psalms	Jeremiah
Leviticus	Proverbs	Lamentations
Numbers	Ecclesiastes	Ezekiel
Deuteronomy	Song of Solomon	Daniel
Joshua		Hosea
Judges		Joel
Ruth		Amos
1 Samuel		Obadiah
2 Samuel		Jonah
1 Kings		Micah
2 Kings		Nahum
1 Chronicles		Habakkuk
2 Chronicles		Zephaniah
Ezra		Haggai
Nehemiah		Zechariah
Esther		Malachi

The Three Kinds of Books in the New Testament

Historical	*Pauline*	*General*
Matthew	**TO CHURCHES:**	Hebrews
Mark	Romans	James
Luke	1 Corinthians	1 Peter
John	2 Corinthians	2 Peter
Acts	Galatians	1 John
	Ephesians	2 John
	Philippians	3 John
	Colossians	Jude
	1 Thessalonians	Revelation
	2 Thessalonians	
	TO INDIVIDUALS:	
	1 Timothy	
	2 Timothy	
	Titus	
	Philemon	

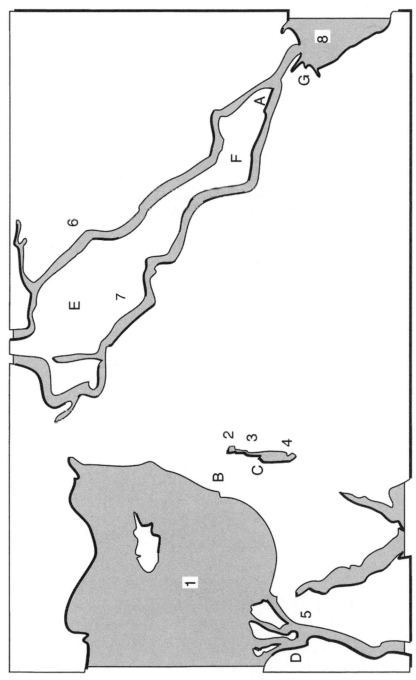

MAP: STATE OF TEXAS/LAND OF THE BIBLE

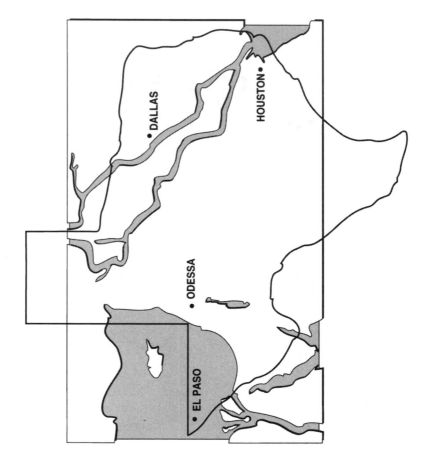

DALLAS

HOUSTON

ODESSA

EL PASO

OVERVIEW OF OLD TESTAMENT HISTORY

ERA	FIGURE		STORY LINE SUMMARY
Creation	*Adam*	*Eden*	Adam is created by God, but he *sins* and *destroys* God's original *plan* for man.
Patriarch	*Abraham*	*Canaan*	Abraham is *chosen* by God to "father" a *people* to *represent* God to the world.
Exodus	*Moses*	*Egypt*	Through Moses God *delivers* the Hebrew people from *slavery* in Egypt and then gives them the *Law*.
Conquest	*Joshua*	*Canaan*	Joshua leads the *conquest* of the *Promised Land*.
Judges	*Samson*	*Canaan*	Samson and others were chosen as *judges* to *govern* the people for *four hundred* rebellious years.
Kingdom	*David*	*Israel*	David, the greatest king in the *new monarchy*, is followed by a succession of mostly *unrighteous* kings, and God eventually *judges* Israel for her sin, sending her into exile.
Exile	*Daniel*	*Babylonia*	Daniel gives *leadership* and encourages *faithfulness* among the *exiles* for the next seventy years.
Return	*Ezra*	*Jerusalem*	Ezra *leads* the people back from *exile* to rebuild *Jerusalem*.
Silence	*Pharisees*	*Jerusalem*	Pharisees and others *entomb* the Israelites in *legalism* for the next *four hundred* years.

1. Creation	5. Judges
2. Patriarch	6. Kingdom
3. Exodus	7. Exile
4. Conquest	8. Return
9. Silence	
10. Gospel	
11. Churches	
12. Missions	

BODIES OF WATER IN THE GOSPELS

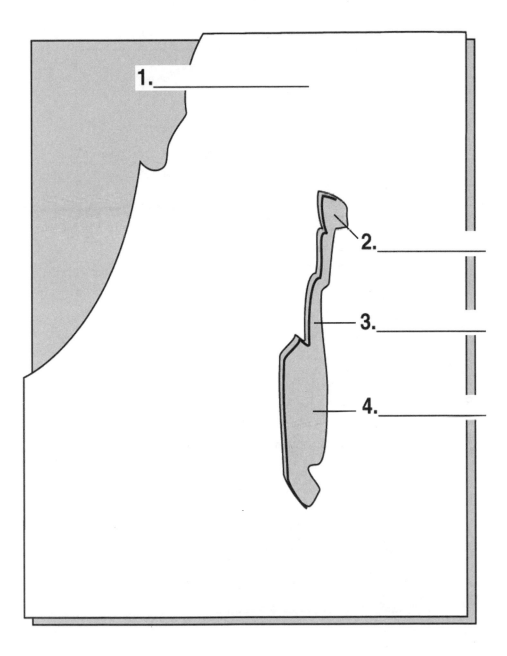

1._____

2._____

3._____

4._____

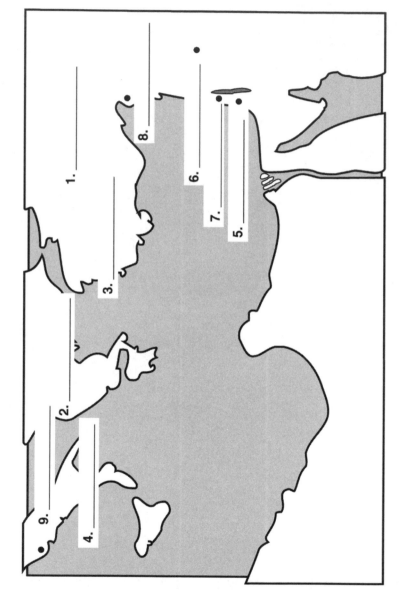

THE GEOGRAPHY OF ACTS

1.

2.

3.

4.

5.

6.

7.

8.

9.

OVERVIEW OF NEW TESTAMENT HISTORY

ERA	FIGURE		STORY LINE SUMMARY
Gospels	Jesus	Palestine	Jesus comes in fulfillment of the Old Testament *prophecies* of a savior and offers *salvation* and the true kingdom of God. While some accept Him, most *reject* Him, and He is crucified, buried, and resurrected.
Church	Peter	Jerusalem	Peter, shortly after the *Ascension* of Jesus, is used by God to *establish* the *Church*, God's next major plan for man.
Missions	Paul	Roman Empire	Paul *expands* the church into the *Roman* Empire during the next two *decades*

TIME LINE OF THE NEW TESTAMENT

Historical Books

A.D. 0	A.D. 30	A.D. 48	A.D. 50	A.D. 53	A.D. 60	A.D. 62	A.D. 67	A.D. 95
	Gospel–Acts					post–Acts		

Pauline Epistles

| | Galatians | 1 Thessalonians
2 Thessalonians | 1 Corinthians
2 Corinthians
Romans | Ephesians
Colossians
Philemon
Philippians | 1 Timothy
Titus | 2 Timothy | |

General Epistles

| | James | | | | 1 Peter
2 Peter | Hebrews
Jude | 1 John
2 John
3 John
Revelation |

MAP OF PALESTINE

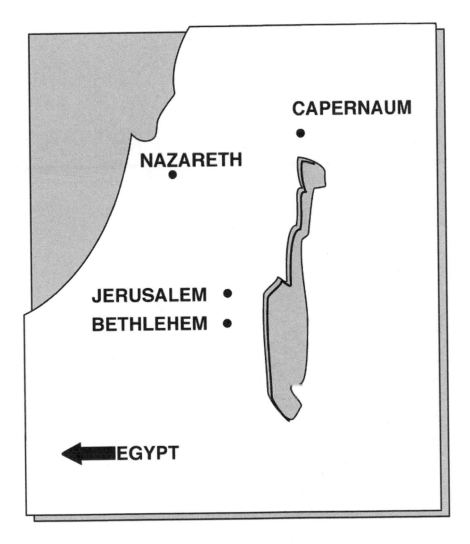

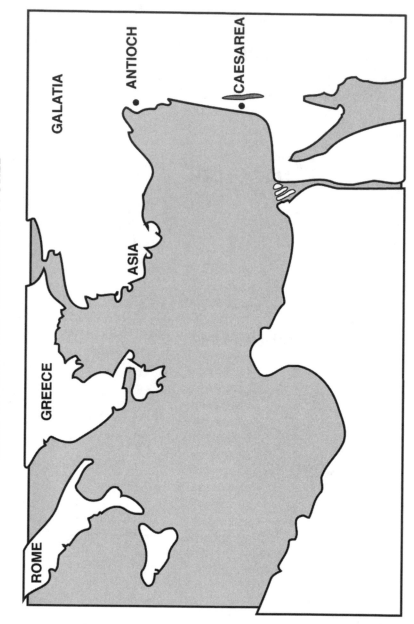

MAP OF THE NEW TESTAMENT WORLD

ROME

GREECE

ASIA

GALATIA

• ANTIOCH

• CAESAREA

Ten Great Doctrines of the Bible

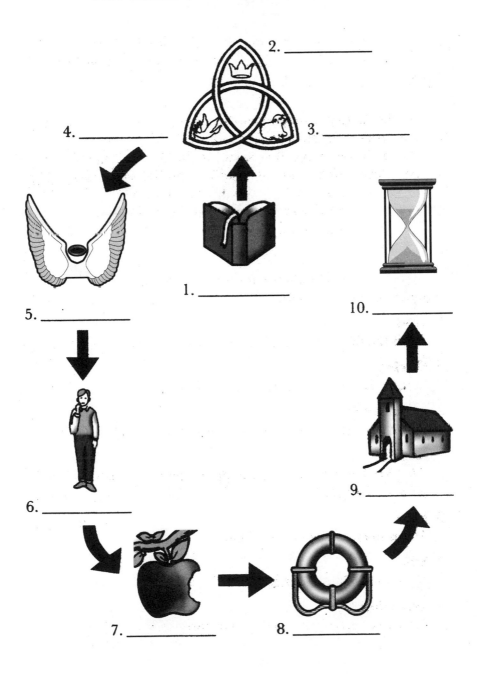

2. _____

4. _____

3. _____

1. _____

5. _____

10. _____

6. _____

9. _____

7. _____

8. _____

The Four Major Subdivisions of the Doctrine of the Bible

 1. Revelation

 2. Inspiration

 3. Illumination

 4. Interpretation

THE FOUR MAJOR SUBDIVISIONS OF THE DOCTRINE OF GOD

 1. Existence

 2. Attributes

 3. Sovereignty

 4. Trinity

THE FOUR MAJOR SUBDIVISIONS OF THE DOCTRINE OF CHRIST

  1. Deity

  2. Humanity

  3. Resurrection

  4. Return

THE FOUR MAJOR SUBDIVISIONS OF THE DOCTRINE OF THE HOLY SPIRIT

 1. Personality

 2. Deity

 3. Salvation

 4. Gifts

THE FOUR MAJOR SUBDIVISIONS OF THE DOCTRINE OF ANGELS

 1. Angels

 2. Demons

 3. Satan

 4. Defenses

THE FOUR MAJOR SUBDIVISIONS OF THE DOCTRINE OF MAN

 1. Origin

 2. Nature

 3. Distinctiveness

 4. Destiny

THE FOUR MAJOR SUBDIVISIONS OF THE DOCTRINE OF SIN

 1. Nature

 2. Fall

 3. Corruption

 4. Rebellion

THE FOUR MAJOR SUBDIVISIONS OF THE DOCTRINE OF SALVATION

 1. Basis

 2. Result

 3. Cost

 4. Timing

THE FOUR MAJOR SUBDIVISIONS OF THE DOCTRINE OF THE CHURCH

 1. Universal Church

 2. Local Church

 3. Leadership

 4. Membership

The Four Major Subdivisions of the Doctrine of Future Things

 1. Return

 2. Judgment

 3. Universe

 4. Eternity

REVIEW OF TEN GREAT DOCTRINES AND THEIR SUBDIVISIONS

1. B _____
    R _____
    I _____
    I _____
    I _____

2. G _____
    E _____
    A _____
    S _____
    T _____

3. C _____
    D _____
    H _____
    R _____
    R _____
    4. _____

4. H _____ S _____
    P _____
    D _____
    S _____
    G _____

5. A _____
    A _____
    D _____
    S _____
    D _____

6. M _____
    O _____
    N _____
    D _____
    D _____

7. S _____
    N _____
    F _____
    C _____
    R _____

8. S _____
    B _____
    R _____
    C _____
    T _____

9. C _____
    U _____
    L _____
    L _____
    M _____

10. F _____ T _____
    R _____
    J _____
    U _____
    E _____